Enter Naomi

SST, L.A. and All That...

≠

Joe Carducci

Redoubt Press
Centennial, Wyoming

Enter Naomi
SST, L.A. and All That...

Joe Carducci

Copyright 2007 D. Joseph Carducci
All rights reserved.
ISBN 978-0-9627612-3-2

Cover art by James Fotopoulos
Photograph by Naomi Petersen, courtesy Dave Chandler
Frontispiece photograph: Naomi and Chris Petersen, Palm Springs, Calif., with parents Takeyo and Leroy in reflection, 1969. (LP)
End photograph: Naomi at Jeff Nelson's wedding, 1993. (courtesy JN)

Photographs throughout this book and the icons in the addendum are the property of the Naomi Petersen estate and Chris Petersen, unless otherwise indicated. All rights reserved.
Photo licensing contact: *info@naomipetersen.com*.

Raymond Pettibon's "Helter Skelter" reprinted by permission of STP Pubs.

L.A. Times photograph by Ken Lubas, Nov. 11, 1984, is reprinted by permission of the Los Angeles Times. All Rights Reserved.

Monitor photograph lifted from No Mag #2, is reprinted by permission of Bruce Kalberg. All Rights Reserved.

"Reggie's Plateau" lyrics reprinted courtesy Jack Brewer.

Book construction by Badi Mibiuba
Snowy Range Graphics, Laramie, Wyoming
www.snowyrangegraphics.com

Redoubt Press
Centennial, Wyoming

Contents

Preface...
Los Angeles...   *1*
Yokohama - Simi...   *13*
SSTs...   *17*
Damageds...   *22*
Enter Naomi...   *25*
Rec-Biz...   *48*
Nikon Eye...   *53*
L.A. Cosmology - You Are Here...   *76*
The Peopling of SST...   *82*
Escape from L.A....   *92*
Acknowledgements II...   *115*
East...   *120*
Nineties...   *128*
The Ventriloquist's Muse...   *130*
Portfolio   *133*
In Wonderland...   *162*
Acclimation...   *170*
Indian Summer...   *179*
Demand...   *183*
Coherency Cycle...   *197*
Immer Simi...   *201*
Us...   *204*
Postscript.   *221*

Addendum

Naomi's Letters.   *229*
Naomi's European Tours Journal.   *257*

Acknowledgements

Special thanks for help in the preparation of this book go to the Petersen family, especially Chris who allowed me access to the material his sister left behind and revisited painful memories to answer my questions.

Thanks to the following for recollections, ideas and other help: Tim Adams, Michael Azerrad, Jim Blanchard, Chris Bopst, Alison Braun, Jack Brewer, Eli Brown, Dan Burbach, Dez Cadena, Geri Carducci, Mark Carducci, Matt Carducci, Mike Carducci, Dave Chandler, Byron Coley, Chris Collins, Ed Colver, Steve Corbin, Scott Crawford, Chris D., Mike Davis, Katon De Pena, Chuck Dukowski, Ray Farrell, Jennifer Precious Finch, Michele Flipside, Jim Fotopoulos, Glen Friedman, Suzi Gardner, Marie Gempis-Carducci, Gary Himelfarb, Rob Holzman, Craig Ibarra, Randy Jahnson, Bruce Kalberg, Raenie Kane, Linda Kite, Jenny Lens, Dave Levine, Dave Lightbourne, Ian MacKaye, Dave Markey, Rosetta Mason, Marco Mathieu, Thurston Moore, Monica Moran, Brendan Mullen, Jeff Nelson, Kara Nicks, James Parker, Raymond Pettibon, Guy Pinhas, Bill Plummer, Bucky Pope, Lee Ranaldo, Scott Reeder, Ryan Richardson, Henry Rollins, Kevin Salk, Jane Schuman, Jordan Schwartz, Gary Sisco, Spot, Bill Stevenson, Kelley Thornton, Roger Trilling, Heather Trudnich, Robert Vodicka, Brian Walsby, Merrill Ward, Mike Watt, Scott Weinrich, Jeff Williams.

Thanks to Lindsay Olson and Toni Mosley at Rainbow Photography for photo help, and to Mike Vann Gray, Badi Mibiuba and Eric Brown at Snowy Range Graphics for the design.

Thanks as well to those whose materials are used to illustrate the story. Some I found with Naomi's belongings, some are from my own hoard, and others are on loan. I couldn't identify or reach everyone regarding these materials; hope you understand. Write with any corrections or information you want me to have for subsequent runs.

Finally, thanks always to my parents…

untitled (excerpt)

these are acts
unforgivable

but easily excused

frantic
like the dying fish

calm
like the dying sea

                        Rosetta

Preface

In early 2005 I was re-publishing an earlier book and editing a collection of essays. I expected to illustrate the new book with some photographs and as about half of the collection was music-oriented I intended to use a number of photographs shot by Naomi Petersen during our time together at SST Records. I assumed I would be able to track her down though I hadn't talked to her in almost eight years. Then I heard by chance that she had died in 2003.

    That did not make sense to me – not her death, and not that it had gone unnoticed for that length of time. Though, given the circumstances of our meeting in 1982 there was also the horrible suspicion that this was the other shoe dropping all these years later, and that we who had known Naomi had failed her. I was still in regular touch with some of the SST crew and others who I felt sure would have clued me in on such important news. But hardly anyone knew anything so I thought I would try to track down her family and find out what I could to inform at least those in my email address book, if not spur some music publication to publish a late obituary or some art publisher to issue of collection of her work.

    Once in touch with Naomi's brother Chris, I was impressed with two things: her full storyline most of which was unknown to me, and that her family knew nothing of her life in the music world. So I spent almost two years trying to tell this story for her friends, her family and anyone else interested in the story of girl loose in that world in those years. A shorter version of this was up online in late 2005. This is more complete as I have been able to talk to more of her friends and make use of her surviving journals and calendars where she made contemporaneous notes on what she was up to. I also was able to dwell on those years and come up with a better portrait of the context we lived in. So many amazing musicians never got heard – the musician's nightmare – that I don't mind, and I know Naomi would not mind, taking the opportunity to bear some greater witness. It sure wasn't our fault.

    It's been resonant work-year for me. I have to thank Naomi for that, though it began with what felt like a weeklong gut-punch. We used her then to make us look a little better than we were, and I am here using her one more time to do so again. It was really something to wake up at SST every morning in those years knowing we had such people at the company and in the bands. Perhaps all that really needs saying is Naomi Petersen was there.

When I was finishing my first book, Rock and the Pop Narcotic, in 1990 I began to pester her and others for photos. Twenty-five years later I see the many reminders to herself in her hectic 1990 weekly planner to "Get prints made for Joe!" Once I settled on the photos I used she wrote, "Sorry I wasn't a whole lot of help… maybe someday I'll get organized and realize all of what I have…" She never did organize her past work; she was too busy navigating the oncoming world, which for her was coming quick. Jeff Nelson, Ray Farrell, and Henry Rollins each told me they had encouraged her to catalog her photo work and publish a book or build a website when later in her life she seemed dispirited. She did want to earn money from the only thing she really loved, but she was so into the doing that she had little energy or time for the exploitation or the marketing of it, or grabbing the credit for something done. And perhaps the paying gigs the music and publishing industries offered were just too damn boring for her. She would make the time to help Henry or myself when we had books in the works, but that was because we were important to her as friends who had shared something rather amazing with her. I had no complaints.

Still, every time I write about music it's a blues… This book is for Naomi, of course. One is lucky to know someone like her, though she'll add to one's responsibilities…. But it's also for the rest of the girls then too. God bless 'em…

And whoever drove them our way… Well, I suppose being an asshole is its own reward.

I'm still working with Naomi's brother Chris to prep her photography for publication and I continue to be struck by how important her work remains as I look at one cultural moment after another that she chose to freeze in time with her camera. Then I look at the photographs of her I've collected from Jeff, Dave, and her brother Chris, and I have to laugh…

Oh Naomi, what you done!

Joe Carducci
Centennial, Wyoming
April 13, 2007

You always know what she thinks, but she does all her feeling alone.

> Zelda Fitzgerald, 1925

Under the slogan, FOR A NEW ART, FOR A NEW REALITY, the most ancient superstitions have been exhumed, the most primitive rites re-enacted...

> Harold Rosenberg, 1960

"The friendly fire has made the sexual revolution a battle."

> Raymond Pettibon, 1986

0. Los Angeles

"'What you're lookin' for is a plain gray frame building just off Hollywood Boulevard on Cahuenga Avenue.... It's called the Waterhole.'

Cowmen from every Western state, from Texas, Canada and even the northern states of Mexico, made their way to the Waterhole...

Regardless of the trail he rode to get there, Hollywood's false-fronted, Western-style Waterhole symbolized each man's Last Chance Saloon on a downhill trail of hurt and disappointment, the place where things simply had to get better or he would be set afoot forever. To a cowboy, being grounded was the meanest hand destiny could deal...

When he arrived he was on foot, without a horse or even a saddle to his name. But there he was shown an entirely new, wide-open frontier, one that he would never have recognized as such, although it lay spread out all around him."
    Diana Serra Cary, 1975
    The Hollywood Posse (*Houghton Mifflin*)

≠

"Myrtle and Grell are to come at seven with the car... We motor through Griffith Park. The high mountain road. The two dead rattlesnakes – one still slightly alive. The many, many rabbits. The blue-bird. The great green mountain gullies. We come out on the other side – San Fernando valley. Motor back past golf links and the deer park to Vermont Avenue. Then out Holly Boul to Cahuenga. We go the The Coffee Pot, the new Greenwich Village style inn. Myrtle and Grell's interest. The barracuda tastes of the oil that is in the sea water here. I think of how much Hollywood is getting to be like Greenwich Village, only on a finer scale – more truly charming... Motor back via Santa Monica Boul to La Brea and over. A delightful night. I wish that Helen and I had a machine."
    Theodore Dreiser, June 3, 1921 diary entry,
    The Grove Book of Hollywood (*Grove*)

"In 1922 my father sold our house and lemon grove in Yorba Linda, and we moved to Whittier.... He borrowed $5,000 to buy some land on the main road connecting the growing towns of Whittier and La Habra. He cleared the lot, put in a tank and a pump, and opened the first service station in the eight-mile stretch between the two towns.

The enterprise was an almost instant success, and he soon opened a general store and market. He added a small counter for my mother's home-baked pies and cakes. One of her specialties was angel food cake. She insisted that it was at its best only when she beat fresh outdoor air into the batter before putting it into the oven. I remember her standing outside the kitchen door in the chilly pre-dawn air, beating the batter with a big wooden spoon."
     Richard Nixon, 1978
     RN (*Warner Books*)

"The highballs they had on the beach – and the sun dropping into the Pacific – their underclothes blowing about them and gulls flapping overhead – so far from the war – so far from business – so far from the troubles of the world – with only the enormous sea and the spacious Pacific landscape – living and rejoicing in life among the primordial magnificence of the world. What had he really cared then, what could he ever really care, for politics or society or learning – so long as he had that happy life to go back to, that life of eternal sun – the Pacific at night, not violent against the shore, but insistent and wild like the high sun."
     Edmund Wilson, 1924
     The Twenties (*Farrar, Straus, Giroux*)

"By the end of World War I, as we have seen, the American film industry had come to dominate the world market. For movie makers and movie fans alike, all roads led to Hollywood... By the turn of the twenties, Hollywood had become big business as well, the newest major industry in the United States. Studio stocks began to be listed on Wall Street in 1919, handled by such respected firms as J.P. Morgan and Kuhn, Loeb."
     Arthur Knight, 1957
     The Liveliest Art (*Mentor*)

≠

"We were a world of our own, and outsiders didn't intrude. People tell you that the reason a lot of actors left Hollywood when sound came in was that their voices were wrong for talkies. That's the official story. The truth is that the coming of sound meant the end of the all-night parties. With talkies, you couldn't stay out till sunrise anymore. You had to rush back from the studios and start learning your lines, ready for the next day's shooting at 8a.m. That was when the studio machine really took over. It controlled you, mind and body, from the moment you were yanked out of bed at dawn until the publicity department put you back to bed at night."
    Louise Brooks, 1979
   "The Girl in the Black Helmet" New Yorker

≠

"The first thing to present itself was a slum of Africans and Filipinos, Japanese and Mexicans. And what permutations and combinations of black, yellow and brown! What complex bastardies!"
    Aldous Huxley, 1939
   After Many a Summer Dies the Swan (Avon)

≠

"He reached the end of Vine Street and began to climb into Pinyon Canyon. Night had started to fall....
  But not even the soft wash of dusk could help the houses. Only dynamite would be of any use against the Mexican ranch houses, Samoan huts, Mediterranean villas, Egyptian and Japanese temples, Swiss chalets, Tudor cottages, and every possible combination of these styles that lined the slopes of the canyon.
  When he noticed that they were all of plaster, lath and paper, he was charitable and blamed their shape on the materials used. Steel, stone and brick curb a builder's fancy a little, forcing him to distribute his stresses and weights and to keep his corners plumb, but plaster and paper know no law, not even that of gravity."
    Nathanael West, 1939
    The Day of the Locust (New Directions)

≠

"Under the moon the back lot was thirty acres of fairyland – not because the locations really looked like African jungles and French châteaux and schooners at

harbor and Broadway at night, but because they looked like the torn picture books of childhood, like fragments of stories dancing in an open fire. I never lived in a house with an attic, but a back lot must be something like that, and at night of course in an enchanted distorted way, it all comes true."
                       F. Scott Fitzgerald, 1941
                       The Last Tycoon (*Penguin*)

≠

"*The bombing of Pearl Harbor in 1941 signaled that war efforts would henceforth be bicoastal, even though Chicago and the Midwest in general continued to produce the heavy machines of war. New York's role, which was restricted to shipbuilding, some aircraft construction, and a few defense industries, was modest in comparison to Chicago's, and both were dwarfed by Los Angeles' role. Los Angeles became home to the most lucrative war contracts, especially in the newer technologies associated with airpower.*"
                       Janet L. Abu-Lughod, 1999
                       New York, Chicago, Los Angeles (*Minnesota*)

≠

"*I hung up, went back out on the yard, stood for a long time in the hot sunshine. Beyond was the road leading down to the outfitting dock, flanked by the various shops, dropping off in the blue-gray stretch of the harbor. Off to the left was a row of hulls in various stages of erection, spaced apart by the craneways. Cranes were silhouetted against the sky like long-legged, one-armed spiders, swinging shapes and plates aboard. Over there the workers walked with care. Everywhere was the hustle and bustle of moving busy workers, trucks, plate lifts, yard cranes, electric mules, the blue flashes of arc welders, brighter than the noonday sun. And the noise, always loud, unabating, ear-splitting. I loved it like my first love.*"
                       Chester Himes, 1945
                       If He Hollers Let Him Go (*Signet*)

≠

"Adorno, who wrote the Dialectic of Enlightenment *with Max Horkheimer in Los Angeles during the war, said after his return to Frankfurt years later, 'It is scarcely an exaggeration to say that any contemporary consciousness that has not appropriated the American experience, even in opposition, has something reactionary about it.' In Los Angeles where Adorno and Horkheimer accumulated their 'data',*

the exiles thought they were encountering America in its purest, most prefigurative moment. Largely ignorant of, or indifferent to, the peculiar historical dialectic that had shaped Southern California, they allowed their image of first sight to become its own myth: Los Angeles as the crystal ball of capitalism's future. And, confronted with this future, they experienced all the more painfully the death agony of Enlightenment Europe."
      Mike Davis, 1990
      City of Quartz (Vintage)

≠

"California is a tragic country – like Palestine, like every promised land. Its short history is a fever-chart of migrations – the land rush, the gold rush, the oil rush, the movie rush, the Okie fruit-picking rush, the wartime rush to the aircraft factories – followed, in each instance, by counter migrations of the disappointed and unsuccessful, moving sorrowfully homeward."
      Christopher Isherwood, 1947
      <u>Horizon</u>, The Grove Book of Hollywood

≠

"North through Coldwater Canyon it began to get hot. When we topped the rise and started to wind down towards the San Fernando Valley it was breathless and blazing. I looked sideways at Spencer. He had a vest on, but the heat didn't seem to bother him. He had something else to bother him a lot more. He looked straight ahead through the windshield and said nothing. The valley had a thick layer of smog nuzzling down on it. From above it looked like a ground mist and then we were in it and it jerked Spencer out of his silence.
 "My God, I thought Southern California had a climate," he said. "What are they doing – burning old truck tires?"
      Raymond Chandler, 1953
      The Long Goodbye (Vintage)

≠

"Still, there were moments when Murphy the actor was strangely disconcerted in those scenes where he played Murphy the soldier in moments of desperate combat. 'This strange jerking back and forth,' he told the reporter of The New York Times, 'between make-believe and reality, between fighting for your life and the discovery that it's only a game and you have to do a retake because a tourist's dog

ran across the field in the middle of the battle,' was somehow uncanny, even disloyal to those who were long dead, buried out there in Europe these ten years and more."
    Charles Whiting, 1990
    Hero (*Scarborough House*)

≠

"The L.A. Sheriff's Office hailed from the Wild West days. It was a modern police agency suffused with 19th-century nostalgia....

 Biscailuz joined the Sheriff's Office in 1907. He was half Anglo and half Spanish-Basque.... William Parker took over the LAPD in 1950. He was an organizational genius. His personal style was inimical to Gene Biscailuz's. Parker abhorred monetary corruption and embraced violence as an essential part of police work. He was an alcoholic martinet on a mission to reinstate pre-20th-century morality.

 Biscailuz and Parker ruled parallel kingdoms. Biscailuz's myth implicitly stressed inclusion. Parker co-opted a TV honcho named Jack Webb. They cooked up a weekly saga called Dragnet – a crime-and-severe-punishment myth that ordained the LAPD with a chaste image and godlike powers.
    James Ellroy, 1996
    My Dark Places (*Knopf*)

≠

"They'd moved to the Knickerbocker after the staff at their first hotel, fed up with the noise, the vandalism, and the endless stream of girls coming in and out of the rooms, had asked them to leave. Gene would accept visits from pals like Johnny Cash, Bob Luman, and Eddie Cochran, of course. Also Lefty Frizzell, John Ashley, and the young actor and singer Ricky Nelson... Since they were both teenagers, Ricky and Juvey often hung out together.... One evening... they went down to the parking lot, along with Jimmy Burton... and jumped into the kid's 1957 Plymouth Fury.... They drove around the Sunset strip.... When they stopped at one intersection, a bevy of young lookers recognized Ricky and started screaming and hollering. When the light turned green, Ricky popped the car into first, waved his middle finger in the air, and tore off down the street, wheels squealing all the way."
    Susan VanHecke, 2000
    Race With the Devil (*St. Martin's*)

"Frequent parties took place in Hollywood at a small alleyway house on Melrose Place near La Cienega. Jazz and rock and Elvis were mixed on the reel-to-reel with Arabian music or Bach or Hank Williams, and the sounds of water dripping or toilets flushing, and the banging of a hammer or drumsticks on a sheet of metal. Everyone was stoned and cheap wine flowed by the gallons. Jack Nicholson usually showed up early for the booze and grass, and the sex orgies just happened – no particular cue – blooming on the big old movie-prop couch or on the mattress in the narrow step-down bedroom where the plaster walls were painted with black sunrises and people hanged by the neck and women being skinned alive."
John Gilmore, 1997
Laid Bare (*Amok*)

"Jimmy loved the ocean, the pounding of the surf, the sunlight turning the water into a sheet of blue glass, the good clean smell, but he had never found the time to enjoy it....

Roselli paused and lit a cigarette. He smiled and tapped Jimmy on the shoulder. 'You probably think I've lost my marbles. What do you care about Frank Nitti? Shit, that's ancient history, right?'

'Hell, no, I'm interested in Capone and Nitti, all those guys. I used to read about them when I was just a kid coming up in Cleveland.'

'Well, I might as well get to the point. Have you seen that TV show, The Untouchables?'...

'Nobody pays attention to that shit,' Jimmy said... 'Who cares?'

'I'll tell you, Jimmy. Sam cares, Joe Batters cares, Paul Ricca cares, and I care.... We're going to clip Desi Arnaz, the producer of this show.'"
Ovid Demaris, 1981
The Last Mafioso (*Bantam*)

"I've mentioned Ed Roth several times in the course of this without really telling you about him. And I want to, because he, more than any other of the customizers, has kept alive the spirit of alienation and rebellion that is so important to the teen-age ethos that customizing grew up in. He's also the most colorful, and the most intellectual, and the most capricious. Also the most cynical.... Any style of life is going to produce its celebrities if it sticks to its rigid standards, but in the East a talented guy would most likely be drawn into the Establishment in one way or

another. That's not so inevitable in California."
> Tom Wolfe, 1963
> "There Goes That Kandy-Kolored Tangerine-Flake Streamline Baby," Esquire

≠

Judee and I got loaded on acid a couple of times and went down to Sunset when it was just really wide open down there, '63 or '64. We'd just sit on a wall and watch people go by. It was really a trip, people were selling dope right on the street. It was something else. I'll never forget that. Then around that time, I got busted for LSD. Even though it was still legal at the time. I was the first bust on record. I remember I was across the street from my shop eating lunch and the Narcs came in there and they were trembling, their hands were shaking, they had their guns out. I was kind of laughing because it was funny. But it wasn't that funny in the end."
> Denis Del Giudice, 2005
> Judee Sill "Dreams Come True," (Water)

≠

"[A]lcohol is a natural part of the Watts style; as natural as LSD is around Hollywood. The white kids dig hallucination simply because he is conditioned to believe so much in escape, escape as an integral part of life, because the white L.A. Scene makes accessible to him so many different forms of it. But a Watts kid, brought up in a pocket of reality, looks perhaps not so much for escape as just for some calm, some relaxation. And beer or wine is good enough for that. Especially at the end of a bad day. Like after you have driven, say, down to Torrance or Long Beach or wherever it is they're hiring because they don't seem to be in Watts, not even in the miles of heavy industry that sprawl along Alameda Street, that gray and murderous arterial which lies at the eastern boundary of Watts looking like the edge of the world."
> Thomas Pynchon, 1966
> "Journey into the Mind of Watts," New York Times Magazine

≠

"The Hollywood scene found some unlikely allies in this cultural feud when Andy Warhol and the Velvet Underground came to California in the summer of 1966. 'LA I liked because the degenerates there all stay in their separate suburban houses,' said

Warhol's director Paul Morrissey. 'That's wonderful because it's so much more modern – people isolated from each other. I don't know where the hippies are getting these ideas to "retribalize" in the middle of the twentieth century.' Up in San Francisco, the Velvets clashed with Fillmore proprietor Bill Graham, who called them 'disgusting germs from New York' – this from a man whose ruthless business style came straight off the streets of the Bronx!... Warhol himself claimed that 'vacant, vacuous Hollywood was everything I ever wanted to mould my life into....'"
      Barney Hoskyns, 1996
      Waiting for the Sun (*Bloomsbury*)

≠

"Despite the protest's limited scope, the local newspapers made a meal out of what they dubbed the riot on Sunset Strip. LONG HAIR NIGHTMARE blared out the headline in the <u>Los Angeles Herald Examiner</u>. An editorial in the November 15 [1966] <u>Los Angeles Times</u> closed its eyes to the indiscriminate use of the curfew law, declaring that there were 'no deep-rooted sociological or economic cause for the weekend rioting. Irresponsibility was simply fanned into complete disregard for the rules and standards.'"
      Fred Goodman, 1997
      The Mansion on the Hill (*Times Books*)

≠

"The majority of Manhattan Beach's 35,000 population live in suburbia. This is called The Tree section of town. The minority section facing the sea is called The Sand. The Sand people do not like to be confused with the Tree People. 'We are not suburbia,' the Sand people say.
  Delineations are important.... Here it is perhaps even more crucial not to be confused with those on the other side of the hill, the flatlanders whose turf must ultimately blend with everything across the L.A. plain, clear to industrial Cudahy."
      Michael Fessier Jr., 1970
      (<u>West</u>) <u>Great God Pan</u> 12

≠

"The girls are different, of course, despite the fact that they all seem to lead similar sexual-existential lives.... As Peter Nevard observes, 'They seem to get freakier as you move farther west. By the time you get to the ones on the Coast, New York starts to look very sane.'

'I want to ball all the pop stars. I want to ball 'em and ball 'em and ball 'em, till I come apart.' - A groupie"
    David Freeman, 1970
    "The Making of The Groupie Movie", <u>Show</u>

≠

"I sit here in California, writing these reminiscences in a heavy rain, thinking of the fires and mud slides, and it does seem as if the magic sunny land I knew has been 'struck', like the movie sets it built, and has disappeared overnight, all its genius gone back into bottles, leaving skyscrapers where the orange blossoms used to scent the wind."
    Johnny Mercer, 1976
    Waiting for the Sun (*Bloomsbury*)

≠

"To recapitulate the past forty years of film history, which was in its way a recapitulation of the past two hundred and fifty years of the Enlightenment: they wanted sex but got horror instead."
    E. Michael Jones, 2000
    Monsters From the Id (*Spence*)

≠

"The beauty of the past and the extremely different conceptions of the present seemed to blend together more easily in people's minds over in England. While it seems the reverse should be true, the present was abrading on the past a bit more abruptly here in L.A., although there was not much of an apparent past to deal with in Los Angeles. Father Junipero Serra's Mission. Possibly Americans, Angelinos in particular are more obtuse. The L.A. present is always busy tearing yesterday down. What was the past in L.A. anyway? A photo of Clark Gable riding in a Duesenberg or Hearst castle up the coast, the crypt of a deceased movie star? A 75 year old apartment building? There wasn't much history, so why be conservative about the present?"
    Bruce Caen, 2005
    Sub-Hollywood (*Yes Press*)

≠

"The Ring Record Book says 8/7/76, so that's the date it was: Danny 'Little Red'

Lopez vs. Art Hafey, L.A. Forum.... I had a couple tickets, so I called Bukowski. Sure, why not, it's free, I'm driving, he'll go....

During prelims, this gruff muh-fuh showed a decided compassion for losers – 'C'mon ref, stop it, the kid's helpless' – very touching, actually. When I noted there were no heavyweights on the bill, nobody in fact above welterweight, he grumbled, 'Heavyweights are just big salamis,' a characterization I'll never forget. Before the main event had started, many beers were consumed by us both."
      Richard Meltzer, 2003
      Autumn Rhythm (*Da Capo*)

≠

"Alan McGee (Creation Records, U.K.) called me up one day crying in Hollywood. He says, 'Where's this place gone? I'm at the place where the Doors' recording studio was. It's now a parking lot. All the landmarks that are making rock 'n' roll literature or in the lyrics of my favorite songs are parking lots and mini-malls! What did you guys do? Tear down your past?' 'Yes.'"
      Kim Fowley, 2000
      <u>Ugly Things</u>, Summer 2001

≠

"History's replacement in L.A. wasn't a myth; it was a sales pitch."
      D.J. Waldie, Oct. 19, 1997 <u>Los Angeles Times</u>

≠

"Los Angeles is the capitol of forgetting."
      R.J. Smith, 2006
      The Great Black Way (*Public Affairs*)

≠

"It's wonderful to see how the dreams of the world are somehow organized and manufactured here and this is why I like to be in Los Angeles.... Los Angeles is the city with the most substance here in America."
      Werner Herzog, Apr. 2006
      Henry Rollins Show, IFC

≠

"L.A.: temperate, sunny, ideal for outdoor living. A wide range of options, until they narrow to live or die."

James Ellroy, July 30, 2006 <u>Los Angeles Times</u>

1. Yokohama - Simi

Naomi's parents met at a dance sponsored by the U.S. Army in Tokyo in 1956. Leroy Petersen was serving in Army Intelligence tracking Soviet submarines in the Sea of Japan. Takeyo Kashimura was raised the daughter of a Zen Buddhist priest in Yokohama, though only at 17 did she discover that her real parents had placed her with her wealthier, city-dwelling aunt and uncle. The shock may have primed her to consider such a radical step as marrying an American soldier though each barely spoke the other's language. They married in Japan and this was no small event for Takeyo's family; the war was just ten years over and the occupation had ended only four years earlier. Americans were accepted, though not often loved.

They moved to his hometown where they were again married, and neither was this a small event in Hyrum, Utah where the Petersens, Mormons of Norwegian and Danish derivation, were centered. The newlyweds settled in Logan, where Leroy began teaching art at the State U. They had a son Christopher and moved to southern California in the early sixties so Takeyo would be near other Japanese. They lived first in Wilmington and Carson. For Naomi's birth in 1964 they returned to Japan so she would have dual citizenship and her mother could reconcile with her family. While in Japan for this year Leroy studied *raku* ceramics under Kaneshige, a designated National Living Treasure. Naomi grew up in Tarzana, Reseda, Chatsworth and Simi Valley as her father taught art at Cleveland High in Reseda. Her parents named their daughter well as Naomi is also a Japanese name where it means *above all, beauty*; the western Naomi derives from the Hebrew term for *pleasantness*. Characteristically, Naomi hated her name. (Her middle name, Kay, is a contraction of her mother's name.) Chris tells me that his sister was a popular, involved student at Lawrence Jr. High in Chatsworth (ballet, baseball, girl scouts, good grades...), but found the residual cowboy culture at Simi Valley High in

Ventura County rough going – Simi Valley is separated from the San Fernando Valley by the county line at Santa Susana Pass. Naomi might have passed as Japanese but her hair was auburn; she was what today a far more secure bi-racial Cali kid might refer to with a laugh as a halfie (Japanese usage: *hafu*). Chris and Naomi resisted their mother's attempts to teach them Japanese. Chris writes, "We didn't want to be thought of as foreign kids!"

Naomi caught interest in rock music from her brother. Chris played guitar while they'd sing Beatles songs together.

> "I remember taking her to her first big concert... She sat on my shoulders to watch the Rolling Stones [July 24, 1978, Anaheim Stadium], but she disappeared only to get squashed along on the front fence and had to be pulled out by security." (CP, Aug. 1, 2005)

There's your thirteen year-old Naomi, straight into the fire! Chris found his shaken-up sister later at the Red Cross tent. He also took her to see Queen, Kiss, Cheap Trick and others. Naomi snuck a small instamatic into these shows and I've seen her shots of these bands from the cheap seats.

Laurence Jr. High in Chatsworth was a middle school offering 7th thru 9th grades. Middle schools were a sixties innovation – an attempt to improve the way schoolkids were bundled by age and physical maturity. In 9th grade at Laurence Naomi was class vice president and the large, wide portrait of the Class of '79 shows her sitting front row center next to the class president – a handsome strapping blond B.M.O.C.

Her father Leroy was a popular art teacher and his better students inevitably hung out at their house which was in walking distance and where he had a wheel and a kiln. The move to Simi was meant to draw a clearer line between work and home. I've also seen Naomi's snapshots of the cute boys at school and can imagine those Simi girls' alarm at this exotic interloper. They must have quickly conspired to freeze Naomi out, using what was handy, her racial background.

Naomi entered Simi High as a sophomore. In Emily White's book, Fast Girls (*Berkley*), a study of the slut myth among high school girls, she lists the following as potential triggers of female social banishment – the high school equivalent of human sacrifice: early physical maturity, extrovert, transferring in, ethnic difference, and dyed hair. Naomi was dealt the full house.

I suspect that on seeing Simi Valley High's elite turn on her, first the girls then inevitably the guys – she talked of one hero who even physically pushed her around – she turned on them. If the good people were actually bad, perhaps the bad people might be something other than as advertised as well. Phyllis Chesler, referring to a journalist's report on such branded girls, writes that "her interviewees all described two opposite, lingering reactions: that of never having got over being taunted and ostracized by other girls and that of having become stronger and more creative because of it." (Woman's Inhumanity to Woman, *Plume*)

Punks were a tiny minority in schools in those years and were considered bad people, homos, losers…. In the Los Angeles media the initial goofy portraits of punk-as-freakshow were morphing into alarmed coverage of regular late night duels between punks and police. At Elks Lodge (March 17, 1979) the LAPD riot squad violently cleared the place during the Plugz set; the Wipers, the Zeros and the Go-Gos had already played. The Alley Cats and X didn't get to. I was in Portland then and when the Wipers got back from L.A. Greg Sage told people what he'd seen and I posted a news article about the aftermath in the record shop. Robert Vodicka, who ran New Alliance for SST in the late eighties wrote his M.A. Thesis on Black Flag and L.A. punk:

> "People in the scene almost universally agree that after the Elks Lodge show, the audiences became more violent…. [Chuck] commented on the more cooperative attitude of the bands at Elks Lodge and how the LAPD bashed heads anyway. 'I felt sold out by the bands at Elks Lodge.'"
> (RV, "No Values" 2003)

Vodicka's tracing of Black Flag's approach to such challenges is sharper and more comprehensive than how they were portrayed in the L.A. media (he also characteristically for an SST employee displays a fine ear when he turns to the music itself). Black Flag would play through whatever the cops did until the power was shut off; later they would patch into the mains so the fusebox only shut off the lights while they'd power on through the dark. And they would play through whatever the audience was doing, which also shocked many in the scene and media. Vodicka quotes Tony Reflex of the Adolescents on this individualist autarchy, "It's almost like Ayn Rand gone completely ballistic." From roadie/bad boy Mike Brinson's reasoned perspective,

> "Dude, there can't be any bigger boner for a musician to be wailing on stage when the whole place is getting destroyed. What can be better?" (MB, The Rise and the Fall, #2 2004)

Brinson also discusses how the first punks who could fight turned tables on the hippies and surfers over the course of six months of gigs at the Fleetwood in 1980. In fact the fighting punks had been hippies and surfers, only they liked the new music and were perhaps just looking for a more interesting angle on the kind of trouble they enjoyed. Like other smart, disaffected social rejects all across the Los Angeles plain Naomi would read the hysterical mainstream coverage of punk rock violence in her own perverse way.

Everything changed for Naomi come High School. Chris went off to UCLA and Naomi began to push against her parents' rules. She gravitated to the small punk circle and began to wear black and dye her hair red or purple. In those years doing such was the act of a pariah – one bitter and courageous enough to make the social in-group's judgment visible and throw it back at them. Today, dying one's hair means something else, or nothing at all. She had her brother take her to see the Clash (Palladium, Oct. 11, 1979) and that was a revelation for Chris – not the Clash so much but about his sister. Naomi began to realize that L.A. was *happening* by listening to Rodney Bingenheimer on KROQ and picking up issues of Flipside.

In 1980 Naomi got a car, a job and a camera and commenced what Chris refers to as her "escalated lifestyle." By spring 1981 she'd cross paths with Black Flag.

2. SSTs

Here's a late 1980 <u>Flipside</u> summary of Black Flag/SST's early south bay movements,

> "Black Flag were interviewed on Nov. 27 at their 'business' home in Torrance. The business is SST Electronics, based around Greg's invention of an antenna tuner. The entire band lives and practices here, which is surprising since the place is small and cluttered with poster artwork, magazines, electronic gear and the bands equipment and personal stuff. This place is only one in a long series of homes for them: they started at the infamous Church in Hermosa, moved to the Hermosa Strand, a place called the 'Würm Hole', where minors hung out and thus attracted the Police and the eventual running out of town by the city council. The new place was in Redondo for awhile, but it was expensive so back to the Church only to get evicted, which gave good reason to have a demolition party, and now they are in Torrance." (<u>Flipside</u>, 1980)

There were actually one or two other short-lived addresses in Hermosa and Torrance as well. The principal casualty of all of this moving around was Greg's original enterprise, SST Electronics. Greg had employed members of his band and the Minutemen assembling his radio tuner amps. But its loss probably helped Greg and Chuck convince the others that the band would prevail. They didn't allow band members to work a job, other than at SST. The Minutemen and the Descendents were both anchored to California and Arizona for years because of jobs this or that member couldn't or wouldn't quit.

In spring 1981 Henry Rollins was about to replace Dez Cadena as vocalist for Black Flag; Dez would move to 2nd guitar. The others in the band were Greg Ginn on guitar, Chuck Dukowski on bass, and Robo on drums. The troop at SST also included roadie Mugger, still 17, and sound-man/producer Spot. Dez's friend Dave Claassen soon started making himself useful as he contemplated dropping out of UCLA.

I was at Systematic Record Distribution in Berkeley, hoping to give L.A. another try or else move back to Chicago. But my year in L.A. (1976-7) had convinced me that it wasn't the place to just show up. I wanted a gig this time; I sounded out Jem, the Varese-Sarabande label, and Archie Patterson (Eurock) who was at Greenworld Distribution in Torrance, but there was nothing. Suzi Gardner has written something on her blog about moving to L.A. from Sacramento:

> "I moved to Los Angeles in 1980. I had many different jobs. A bikini dancer, and a stripper. Held down actual office jobs at Cannon Films, L.A. Weekly, and two advertising agencies. I worked at Millie's as a prep cook and food server, on speed in the daytime, and heroin at night for the cleaning part at the end... I've flyered cars in Pasadena on one of the hottest and smoggiest days of the year. I was the girl who answered the phone at a dating service. I did 6 years at United Independent Taxi off and on as an order-taker/backup dispatcher. I cocktail waitressed at the Troubadour, Cathay DeGrande, and did a multi-year stint at world famous Raji's as a sometimes very inebriated waitress. During all of this madness I was lucky enough to live out a Rock & Roll dream." (SG, butteyedigress.blogspot.com, Dec. 11, 2006)

Such chaos wasn't for me, and I didn't want to work at a movie theater or a restaurant again. Talking with Suzi now, even she seems amazed she pulled it off. L7, her dream, didn't end well but I think she's doing okay now.

At one of the last Dez-on-vocals gigs (Tut's, July 15, 1981 – Chicago) I offered to move down and run the SST office; Greg took me up on my offer though he laughed that they didn't really have an office and they also had no money – *Sounded good to me!* I had happened to call down to SST the month before, just as the Torrance P.D. burst into the office so I gathered things could be unusual around SST – Spot answered any question I asked with nervous laughter and "Ahhh... I don't know!" while he watched the cops ransack the place. (They were always expecting to find narcotics; Jem told them that the LAPD had once come in right after they'd dropped off records and opened up all the boxes.) Spot finally handed the phone to Mike Watt who whispered to me what was going on. Black Flag had just left for the tour, and Spot tells me he was to catch up to them after wrapping up production work on either Black Flag, Minutemen, Saccharine Trust,

Overkill, Stains, Descendents, Necros, or Fix – he doesn't recall which. He closed down Torrance SST, secured tapes in storage, sold enough Black Flag records to buy a one way ticket to Newark just as the band was deciding between Dave Slut and Henry Rollins as the new singer.

On their return to L.A. at tour's end, SST was a bank of three pay-phones near Beverly & Western in what is now Korea-town. I asked Chuck what doing business on the street was like:

> "Once I got started I just grooved and kinda enjoyed what was good about the situation: outside, stuff going on, ya know. I don't remember anyone recognizing me except the people who lived at the Oxford hse around the corner, where we were staying... Merrill, Malissa and a load of other people lived there." (CD, Feb. 6, 2006)

Chuck's and the others' ability to roll with anything and enjoy it no matter how goofy, embarrassing or dangerous, was one of the fundamental building blocks of Black Flag and the SST approach.

Settling on the Unicorn studio in West Hollywood to record the "Damaged" album, the band also rented the rear offices to live and practice in. One of the first things I did in L.A. that Sept. was meet up with promoter Mike Sheppard. I had helped him put on the San Francisco date for Throbbing Gristle/Flipper/Church Police at Kezar Pavilion (May 29, 1981). Mike insisted that on my return to L.A., he must buy me a Tommy's chili-burger (never mind he owed me five hundred, not five bucks – I'm cool). So we stood at a counter open to the parking lot and ate a sandwich the likes of which were then impossible to come by in those sophisto realms north along the coast. The food Angelinos grab at Oki-Dog, Pink's or nameless diners, taquerias, char-broiled burger stands, and taco trucks might fly in the face of nutritional science and hippie-vegan ethics but they like it and know the best places and are up for checking out any new start-up.

In the van Black Flag threw empty coffee cups and orange juice bottles down onto the rocker panels; when they stopped somewhere they simply kicked the garbage into the street. Trashing? Graffiti-ing? Postering? Pissing? Los Angeles seemed the fallen dream of generations of transplants; the locals, now acclimated to its harsh scape didn't see the point in taking care of it. It took care of itself. It just *was*. And this was quite unlike other cities. It was part of what made punks in the rest of the country feel like naïve goo-goo hippies when the L.A. bands rolled up.

Sheppard was to begin booking for SST but never showed. The idea was that upon the release of "Damaged" and now packing Henry on vocals, Black Flag would tour forever, and booking from the road especially in the days before email, cell phones, faxes and answering machines was virtually impossible. When I asked Chuck where Sheppard was, he put thumb and finger to lips and inhaled – the international sign for "pot-head." Chuck continued booking with help from Irving Plaza's Chris Gremsky in New York, and a bit later Jordan Schwartz, who was doing a fanzine called We Got Power.

One minute Jordan was grousing about "those hippies at SST" and the next minute he was one of 'em. At the website (wegotpowerfilms.com) you can see these early issues and read Spot's "In praise of Neo-bopism," see a photo of myself with Mugger and Rob Holzman (then Saccharine Trust's drummer) taken the first week I was down, and an ad Chuck put together for the first Minutemen and Saccharine Trust albums touting as well my fictitious line of clothing ("Carducci – The Man, The Shirt"). Mugger told me Greg and Chuck had prepared everyone that I was likely a pot-head myself since I was into Flipper and didn't shave; that I wasn't made my fit all the easier. At that point Black Flag were basically drug and alcohol free – certain allowances were made for Dez. In a great issue of the SF mag Damage (#11, Dec. 1980) wherein they put focus on the L.A. scene, the senior editor Jonathan Formula sits down with Slash editor Claude Bessy (RIP), Debbie Dub, and Greg Ginn in an Irish bar in the Mission District and they're all drinking Guinness except Greg and his coffee.

Another distinguishing characteristic of Los Angeles, especially for this small town Midwestern boy, were the young girls that would show up at the gigs. SoCal seemed full of broken families, and the loosed kids fully mobile. They might be as young as 13 when they began to float around the city, traveling in cars driven by older friends. The hip girl from crosstown might show up at the gig with some sullen zit-faced metaller-with-a-car who collected his blowjob and was off. The Southland was lit up by Rodney Bingenheimer, KROQ simulcasting, Flipside's canvassing the punk nightlife, and Black Flag playing and promoting everywhere. Punks in L.A. high schools were soon not so tiny a minority.

Black Flag shows were far-flung into all corners of greater L.A., and such was the hunger for music we could stand, that gigs in San Diego, Phoenix and San Francisco were often treated as local shows. In 1982, before Davo was part of the roadcrew, Black Flag was out touring and he heard Rosetta and I comparing notes on how great the Toiling Midgets were. Rosetta had just heard from up north and knew they were playing that night, so Davo said, "Let's go." He drove us the 400 miles to SF. We made the gig, said hello to friends who thought we were nuts because up there they don't leave "The City" for nothing, and then drove right back down to L.A. Davo *The Drivah!* in training – he later logged more miles than anyone south of the space program as he drove for Black Flag, Firehose, and the Meat Puppets; hope he's doing okay.

At one of the Cuckoo's Nest gigs in Costa Mesa (probably Sept. 26, 1981: Subhumans/CH3/Circle One/Detours/whoever), the opener's singer was nervously being cool with the mic-stand and the base unscrewed and knocked a girl out cold; Greg was the only one who ran to help her. We stopped at the Ginns' house in Hermosa Beach for the night. It was dark and in memory it doesn't seem the same place I knew later; we slept in some kind of storage area, bigger than the shed Henry later moved into. Driving back up to West Hollywood in the van the next morning, Henry and I, the newbies, listened as Mugger told some crazed sex story about one of his feral buddies. I commented, "Everyone's a little randier out here." Henry, who I did not yet know, looked over and said "Yeah!" like he'd noticed. Chuck said something about American social geography and Darwinian anthropology. A year or so later, sitting around SST-Phelan in Redondo, Chuck summarized his biology-based version of Hobbes' All Against All, to which Greg responded, "Yeah, but there's friends." See Chuck's song, "My War" for his response. Friends... Enemies... Male. Female. Thesis/Antithesis. All proved true under the L.A. sun.

3. Damageds

Black Flag's "Damaged" album seemed cursed. Many of the songs had already been recorded three times with three different singers (Keith, Ron/Chavo, and Dez) and plans had once been to see it released on Upsetter Records, the label owned by Chris D. (of <u>Slash</u> magazine and bands the Flesheaters and Divine Horsemen). Black Flag were also informally managed for a short while by Marshall Berle, who had signed Van Halen to Warners, managed the Alleycats, and happened to be Uncle Miltie's nephew. Now with Henry, Spot and the band re-*re*recorded the album at Unicorn which was near the Tropicana on Santa Monica Blvd. The Tropicana's diner was called Duke's and we ate there when Greg had cash. I saw Jodie Foster in the place once, and somebody in there actually asked me if I was Jack Nicholson. (I must've been wearing shades and he must've been high.) When the Plasmatics were in town for their big punk rock car-demolition showcase Henry stared a hole through the head of their blue-mohawk-ed guitarist while he tried to swallow his waffle.

When "Damaged" was finally finished, Spot recorded the Meat Puppets' first album there at Unicorn. The Kirkwood brothers ate mushrooms and then couldn't play unless they faced each other right in front of Derrick's drums; the leakage was such that in the mixing you could push and pull the faders all you wanted and nothing changed – you had to eq the drum tracks to change the guitar sound! Their manager, Laurie, had warned Spot there was no telling what they might do so Spot set up a secondary mix straight to a two-track at the slow speed that caught everything the multi-track didn't – the best tracks on the album as it happened.

Unicorn also was a label that somehow had MCA distribution. It was owned by a bottle-blonde from Israel named Daphna. (There's a pic. of her with Black Flag on pg. 28 of Henry's book, Get in the Van, 2nd ed., 2.13.61) She was making a suicide run at the charts with albums by a German pop star, an Argentine new wave duo, and the second engineer on some Pink Floyd album. MCA was going to dump the label anyway but their president thought he might cadge some moral cred within the industry (!) by pinning it on his supposed objections to the "Damaged" album. Variety's headline for September 24, 1981 read, "'Moral' Reasons Given for Album's Rejection By MCA," and the story had it that "(MCA Distributing Corp. prexy Al Bergamo) noted that, as a father of daughters, he felt uncomfortable about handling the band."

Daphna worked the dust-up to cover her own tracks and made MCA look like EMI re the Sex Pistols, but in the end Unicorn found itself distributed via the Pickwick group. Unfortunately, we threw the "Damaged" album into this pipeline; we almost threw everything into it: Minutemen, Saccharine Trust, Meat Puppets... Unicorn was a wide-open sugar trap right down to the orgy in Daphna's Mulholland Drive mansion, which I slept through.

Laurie O'Connell of the band/art-project Monitor/World Imitation was the Meat Puppets' manager and somehow this led her to the receptionist's job at Unicorn. Laurie was part of a circle that included writer-artist Boyd Rice, painter Jeffrey Vallance, and musician Fred Nilsen (B People, Los Angeles Free Music Society) – a very influential fount of ideas, music and art whose brains were picked by everyone from Devo to Throbbing Gristle. Look for a Boyd Rice documentary from Larry Wessel soon. In issue 1 (and perhaps 2) of The Colonial Rick Potts of the Human Hands tells the story of L.A.F.M.S. He recalls his CalArts cronies responding with "mixed annoyance" to Le Forte Four's 1974 album and how they graduated to Poobah's Records in Pasadena where they learned loads from owner Jay Green and staffer Tom Recchion (Doo-dooettes, Bpeople).

I was pleased to have arranged this collision of Laurie's neo-hippie/dada scene with the marauding *art brut* of Black Flag. Laurie was rather bemused herself I think. She took Teresa, one of the floating young girls, under her wing for this short while. Teresa was thought to be a girl Black Flag had once run across and remembered as Vaseline Woman, though she proved to be another girl entirely thus earning the distinction of being called by her name. (Other memorable handles assigned to members of the girl parade: Coughing Disease Woman, Tomato Juice Woman, Duct Tape Woman, Crusty Christie...) Laurie compared SST to a locker room, though she smiled as she said it. Her marriage to Steve Thomsen, the quiet genius behind Monitor/W.I., was then foundering on the rocks of the Meat Puppets' Curt Kirkwood. Curt was then living on bee pollen and Laurie said they'd gone out to the desert, dropped acid and made prolonged eye-contact until they saw the animals they had always been. No locker room, that.

Meanwhile, just outside SST on Santa Monica Blvd the hustlers stared into traffic two to a block until dawn; the girls worked Sunset. You could sell blood at the Red Cross office on Melrose; there was a line forming every morning before they opened. Somewhere out there was Greg's ex-girlfriend, Medea, who was part of the band's early Hermosa Beach braintrust. She can be glimpsed behind the band with Spot and Greg's brother Raymond Pettibon in the 1979-80 Black Flag interview segment of the film, "The Decline of Western Civilization." Medea was Mexican, in the parlance, and brought graffiti and a street-smart fearlessness into the operation; when the cops mobilized to track down the Black Flag graffiti-perps she tagged the station. She was a tough, broken girl ultimately lost to the street; see her song, "Room 13" on the "Damaged" album wherein she essentially commands of Greg to keep her alive, over and over. (This singular lyric has never been sung by a woman which makes it Medea's creepy crawl of Black Flag and men in general; on the West Memphis 3 benefit album, "Rise Above," it's sung by the Slipknot dude, not Exene.) Greg's answer songs include "Life of Pain" (first line: *"Look what you've done to your arms!"*), and "Bastard In Love," wherein he insists that his love is real, over and over. SST was something more than a locker room.

4. Enter Naomi

In late 1981 it was still a few months before "colonic irrigation" ads in the L.A. Weekly warned, "Death begins in the colon," and two years before the naming of the Aids virus and a final ending of what we refer to as The Sixties – begun with the election of young Kennedy, the introduction of the Pill, and the court-ordered removal of crucifixes from public schools. None of which were as advertised: Young tan handsome JFK had one foot in the grave even before our anti-hero avatar fired off the starter pistol on the hippie era; Nixon lived to be 81. In a 1957 article in Pageant magazine on the development of the Pill the zeitgeist itself was promising that "a new contraceptive pill seems to answer all the objections on physical, psychological and moral grounds." And all these years later the public school systems seem well without a prayer despite at least ten cycles of reform that accomplish little but teachers' union culpability evasion.

Thurston Moore called punk a nihilist hippie movement. Maybe in the end punk was simply the nihilist phase of hippie. In novelist and Kesey traveling companion Robert Stone's recent memoir he writes,

> "By 1970, there may have been more in the way of threat than promise around. There was a sense in which everybody lost, or at least paid his or her way. The middle Americans, shocked at seeing hysterical rage visited by half-educated youth on their flag, the radical folkies in flat woolly caps appalled to hear Bob Dylan zap out those electric chords at Newport – all were seeing the future of their dreams go down." (RS, Prime Green, *Harper Collins*)

In a Louis Menand essay called "The Stone Age – Drugs and Rock'n'Roll," he has it that,

> "After the Altamont concert disaster in December 1969... psychedelia lost its middle-class appeal. More unpleasant

> news followed in 1970 – the Kent State and Jackson State shootings, the Manson Family trials, the deaths by overdose of famous rock stars. And even more quickly than it had sprung up, the media fascination with the counterculture evaporated. But the counterculture, stripped of its idealism and its sexiness, lingered on."
> (LM, American Studies, *Farrar, Straus and Giroux*)

Punk was what was left when Hippie found it had been wrong. Few confessions or admissions were forthcoming but in general the revolution was dropped for righteous-flavored entrepreneurship and connoisseurship – that or retirement to academe. Punk surely pre-dated Hippie but its surly pessimism had been a blue collar affair until middle class wise-guys needed a language to dispense with the mass success of sixties shopkeep sellout that began in what we refer to as The Seventies. Shopkeep went corporate very fast – the record industry, the radio business, and <u>Rolling Stone</u> of course, but Starbucks, Celestial Seasoning, Sam Adams, Nike, Apple, Microsoft and more date from this period too. And only post-Hippie did Punk develop something like a media voice, though it was never a mass media voice.

Punk felt itself without illusions, and was determined to proceed without lies or even mere politesse. One early reviewer of Clinton Heylin's new punk history, Babylon's Burning (*Cannongate*), admires it but is disappointed with the smallness of what he claims is its summary point on Punk's philosophy: to live without lies. But there's nothing small about that ambition; it is, in fact, a civilization-wrecker. And for the women and girls involved?! (btw, the Heylin book includes seven Naomi shots in UK ed.)

But actually, Clinton writes,

> "Not my summary point at all. Punk was about either redeeming rock or destroying it, the honesty was a by-product of these things." (CH, March 14, 2007)

He goes on to guess that the reviewer was responding to Richard Hell who is quoted in the book:

> "[The punk ideal] is so ambitious it can't be maintained. It has such a level of intensity – it had to do with a kind of honesty that's so pure that it doesn't really exist; so it's going to destroy you if you try to [maintain] it."
> (RH, Babylon's Burning, *Cannongate*)

Photographer Jenny Lens, who shot L.A. punk from 1976 to 1980, was an advisor on the Germs feature film, "What We Do Is Secret," and writes in her blog that she was outraged by the cavalier nonsense and misrepresentation in the film. When told she needed to learn to lie, she answers, "NEVER!"

In Los Angeles, where hippies had originally referred to themselves as freaks, perhaps these eras "blended seamlessly" as writer James Ellroy claims. However, on Dec. 7, 1980, when Darby Crash died, at least one south bay hippie must've been caught out laughing, because the next day when John Lennon was killed on the other side of the country, that hippie went to the famous punk rock recording studio Media Art in Hermosa Beach and fired his gun up the stairwell in protest.

In Legs McNeil and Gillian McCain's great oral history, Please Kill Me (*Penguin*), the Ramones don't enter the narrative until page 175. First we get testimonies that begin in 1965 about Warhol, the Velvet Underground, the Doors, MC5, the Stooges, the New York Dolls, Patti Smith Group, and Television. McNeil's fanzine, <u>Punk</u>, begun with cartoonist John Holmstrom in 1975 under the influence of the first Dictators album ("Go Girl Crazy," 1975), christened the sensibility at least ten years into its NYC life. Please Kill Me is not often sentimental or romantic, even as its once young, vibrant characters begin to withdraw or drop dead, but there are notably awestruck digressions involving Holmstrom meeting <u>Mad</u> magazine founder Harvey Kurtzman, the Stooges' Ron Asheton's visits to an elderly Larry Fine of the Three Stooges at the Motion Picture Rest Home, and especially the Dolls/Heatbreakers' Jerry Nolan's recollection of seeing Elvis Presley in 1957, with which the book ends:

> "I was in the third row, as close as you could get. You could almost touch him.... I had never seen anyone put on a show like that. I was almost embarrassed. It was just shocking.... I could see that his shoes were worn out. Maybe they were just his favorites and he didn't want to quit wearing them. But I also had a tinge of pity, thinking maybe he was poor. But I dug it...
>
> That show, even at ten years old, really changed my life. I was overwhelmed by Elvis. I was overwhelmed by the musicians. I could feel the playing."
> (JN, Please Kill Me, *Penguin*)

Punk then, seemed made by the nominal adults in the last years of coherent American working class culture, adult-kids who took advantage of that coherence and these new years of extended adolescence that our society's post-war science and wealth allowed. The earlier model of bohemia required slumming elites. Burroughs was the dissolute scion of a family fortune; Kerouac was not.

Come Punk, the wise-ass lumpen-hipsters remade the junk-culture of their childhood into a sophisticated but reflexively, corrosively unpretentious, unpolitical, funny, absurd, even inert provocation. In Jon Savage's definitive chronicle of the Sex Pistols, rock writer Nick Kent tells the story of Malcolm McLaren's managerial dry run with the New York Dolls in NYC – he and Vivienne Westwood dressed them in red leather Soviet kitsch:

> "After the show [Feb. 28, 1976] Lisa Robinson came backstage. She thought Malcolm was mad. She rounds on JoHansen, 'What is this Communist shit?' who, being the old trouper that he is, says 'It ain't nuthin' serious, y'know'. Malcolm was looking at him and thinking, 'You bastard', because Malcolm *was* serious. Lenny Kaye went over to Thunders and asked him the same question. Much to Malcolm's delight, Thunders said: 'What's it to ya?' Malcolm would tell this story over and over again...."
> (NK, England's Dreaming, St. Martin's)

McLaren had Paris 68er ambitions but he'd settle for punk belligerence. And in truth each and every Sex Pistols media outrage in the years that followed was due to the freed loutish behavior of the lads in the band, rather than the carefully engineered spectacles of the McLaren brain-trust, which were supposed to heighten the contradictions of late period capitalism blah blah.... (Meanwhile socialism collapsed!)

I was always partial to Rik L. Rik's quote from 1979, which was disseminated in Posh-Boy press material, "There's no set political philosophy with the punks now. The only thing unifying them is Quaaludes," and Gary Panter's cover for <u>Slash</u> (Aug. 1979) where his lumpen everypunk Jimbo proclaims, "The world don't deserve this good of a magazine!!!" or any number of Pettibon drawings – how about the hippie captioned, "I started wetting the bed again in 1967," or the bloody knife-wielding hippie surrounded by scattered, severed limbs captioned, "Somebody lit up a joint."

And Punk, or Hippie, or whatever it was, was never more nihilistic than as it expired unnoticed in the mid-80s buried beneath the ascension of more purely middle class college-based hardcore, alt-rock, indie, jamband scenes. And yet, there are no nihilists – just people, kids...

Naomi was troubled, and so were we all; she fit right in.

I remember a commotion one night in November 1981 in the SST offices behind Unicorn. I still barely knew the guys but there was suddenly sex in the air – Mugger made a great barometer. He said laughing, "Come on, Carducci!" I ignored him and continued working on what was my first task, collating the media, distribution, and retail information I brought with me from Systematic with what SST had amassed and copying it into four useable rolodexes. I looked up and saw only the outline of a girl following the band through to the practice room and did not inquire further, but I now know that was Naomi.

Black Flag left for Houston and the beginning of their "Damaged" tour on Nov. 26, 1981; they returned to L.A. to headline the big New Year's Eve Olympic Auditorium gig (BF/Blasters/Suburban Lawns/ Fear/Saccharine Trust). In Naomi's calendar she marks Jan 3, 1982 "Find out Robo is stuck in Cuba!" and Jan. 5, "First time talk to anybody since Nov. 25th." She begins a painting of D. Boon on the 8th, writes a letter to Greg on the 9th, and on the 16th "get letter from <u>Dez</u>!" In February she works more on the D. Boon, calls SST talks to Greg on the 8th, Mugger on the 18th ("who was nice for him"). Worried they might despise her she seems convinced they don't. On April 14th she drives down to SST, now in Redondo, and shows her D. Boon painting, "They love it! Esp. Chuck!"

There was something of a toll that women or girls paid when they got next to Black Flag. But that expectation was what they as females intuited from a Black Flag performance. It was a little different at home in Los Angeles where the band was approachable under more normal conditions and better behaved; this argues for Naomi's agency no matter how drunk she may have been. On tour it was Mugger who beat the drum for girls who wanted to meet the band in the short hours between load-in and load-out at the club. A classic picture of this was painted by the revolutionist Texas band, M.D.C., in <u>Maximum Rock 'n Roll</u>, wherein the complaint lodged ran along the lines: You listen to Black Flag's records and it's all pain and anger and then they show up in your town, pile out of their van and go, "Dude, where are the broads? Get it happening!"

In Spot's liner notes for the "Everything Went Black" compilation of early Black Flag recordings (required reading), he recounts his own first impressions of Greg as "someone totally out of step with the sunshine and the surf and the skateboards." The band was full of high school losers – a perverse mix of brainy types and manic physical ones. The brainy took courage from the fearlessness of the physical ones, and the physical learned from the brainy to be smarter about applying their energy. Within music they found, in classic south bay surfer-boho fashion, that in simply deciding to live as if the hierarchies around them did not exist they created a sexy anti-glamour for themselves. Interesting girls with their own struggle against these hierarchies would respond. These girls' numbers alone got Black Flag run out of Torrance. That era's "Jealous Again" EP has Pettibon art that features Miltown High Cowgirl likenesses of Medea and Tertia dueling over letter-man Chuck! The "Six Pack" 45 banding messages scratched into the vinyl are "Torrance tang / It's happening!"

In the early eighties the members of Black Flag were still, say, a couple years from having their high school ids sated. Once the touring got serious after "Damaged" (a tour might be 58 dates in 60 days, two weeks in Europe, and then another 58/60 in smaller towns) the relative merit of sleep rose versus sex, though even then the stars might align every few weeks and the gig, the audience, the crashpad, the girls would come together and the band would get back to Redondo talking about Richmond, or Chicago, or some other memorable vortex of rock/exhaustion/hunger/sex/insanity. Often for the girls it was a simple matter of exploring the world in the short years before settling down. Touring musicians likely have always seemed to local girls to be men apart – exciting, in touch with their feelings, unsullen, unstuck, etc., and even if they prove a disappointment they are immediately gone and a girl needn't worry about having to avoid them around town. But in Naomi's case, even at seventeen, she was on a trajectory of her own devising; she was going to be seeing a lot of these musicians.

Spot termed the Black Flag crew back then as "one of the most difficult societies to crack." He first noticed Naomi when she managed to get herself inside the van after one of the gigs in late 1980 or early '81...

> "Nothing more than Naomi tagging along with us for a ride that either got her closer to home or the next party that night. She was in a very gabby, happy mood.... I seem to recall that some folks were bumming on her, but that was standard m.o. among the troop those days... She was not

> wearing the usual black; somehow I remember a white, light
> or brightly colored party type dress (y'know, that kinda retro
> punker-in-petticoats look) with the contrasting black hair
> and dark makeup. Something about her stood out in the
> dark confines of the van." (S, Jan. 21, 2006)

I myself first noted her as the stylish Asian-looking girl at a gig at the Cuckoo's Nest (likely Oct. 3, 1981: Black Flag/Red Cross/Meat Puppets). She would have driven over sixty miles from her home in Simi Valley through Los Angeles to get to this good-sized Orange County club.

Black Flag at this point was unable to play in L.A. due to the LAPD's excessive interest, and they were playing smaller, outlying mailing list- and locally- promoted gigs so as to keep the new line-up in gear for the coming "Damaged" tours. Henry wrote up a couple of these pick-up gigs for Black Flag's "Creepy Crawler" newsletter:

> "[W]e played a party with the Descendents and the
> Subhumans Friday night [Sept. 18, 1981]. They played great
> sets (may I add that this was all going on in the kitchen)....
> We played a few songs and then went into 'DAMAGED I'. I
> broke the mike, so I had to scream real loud. I put my head
> through the wall.... I didn't realize the Cops came in. I turn
> around, there they are.... Some friends grabbed me and got
> me out of the house and threw me in a car. Earl from
> Saccharine Trust was not as lucky. He got chased, hurdled a
> fence, fell and broke his leg in three places, lost 5 or 6 teeth
> and a good part of his lower lip. Me, Greg, Mugger and
> Pettibone went to see him today and he seems to be in good
> spirits." (HR, Creepy Crawler III)

And,

> "Yesterday we played an outside gig at San Pedro High
> School [Oct. 20, 1981]. We set up on the school steps. Class
> Break came around and everybody poured out to see us play.
> We got thru 1 song and the PA broke. So we went into
> 'DAMAGED I' with no mike. We did a 25 minute version of
> it with me running around screaming.... The usual gig these
> people would see does not contain the lack of respect for
> form and presentation. One interesting thing was that
> nobody moved. They stayed still, and also, everybody – long
> hair, short hair, stoner, surfer, cheered and yelled and enjoyed

themselves. This is the first high school that we've successfully played." (HR, Creepy Crawler IV, Oct. 1981)

Naomi stood out at the Cuckoo's Nest because the O.C. punk rabble was young, sullen and largely white and male. She can be seen in an Ed Colver shot in Get In the Van (pg. 24 of the 2nd edition, top shot, bottom left, half-obscured). When I saw her there she wore dark sharkskin bouffant skirts and black blouse and sweater – very girlish except for all that black on black. Knowing nothing about her, my first impression was that a guy could get lost in all those ruffles, layers and black. The few other girls there were either slack beach girls or O.C. punkettes with far less flair. At one point between bands, Scranny, Wasted Youth's singer ran up to the microphone and apropos not much ordered the kids to "Destroy this place!" (Black Flag often found itself shoring up beleaguered entrepreneurs by deliberately crossing punk rock boycotts: the Posh-boy label, promoter Dirk Dirksen in SF, and here, promoter Jerry Roach.) The crowd ignored Scranny; they wanted to see Black Flag play, wanted to see this new singer, Henry Rollins. Scranny, perhaps did not; he trudged back up the office stairwell and lumped it and the raging performance that followed. Henry was going to work out, needless to say.

Mugger told me later that this girl Naomi was Robo-scam, which for Mugger constituted discretion. I nodded thoughtfully at this information, no doubt. Spot thinks that Naomi was no-one's scam until the night up behind Unicorn. Robo was almost thirty then; he spoke English with a heavy Colombian accent, and with his military bearing you easily heard his curt imperatives barked at the kids (Mugger, Bill Stevenson). Everyone's favorite was the commanded question, "Mugger, why you space out?!" There would be a pause, and then he would repeat, "WHY!?" and the clipped cadence and the accent seemed juiced by an cosmic bleat of abject incomprehension. The first job I saw them tackle was the rebuilding of the van conversion to accommodate Dez's guitar amp now that the band was a five piece. They did this outside of Unicorn on Santa Monica Blvd; I was impressed.

Naomi had a very good ear for music and though this alone might explain her attraction to Black Flag-SST, I also think the casual mixed provenance of our scene looked inviting to her. At the gigs you saw this, while if all you did was read the papers you'd think Black Flag was the leading edge of young white suburban racism – what a joke... Other than the greats at <u>Slash</u> magazine (Claude Bessy – RIP, Chris D., Jeffrey Lee Pierce – RIP...) and Richard Meltzer at the <u>L.A. Reader</u>, music writers in those early years simply did not speak contemporary *Los Angeles* – the Germs, X, and others up to N.W.A., had similar problems.

New Yorkers and Londoners thought of their cities as cosmopolitan immigration-fortified cities-of-the-world with great restaurants; how could writers there grasp from their hard-won niches in those vertical hierarchies the easy, open, horizontal drive-thru future spreading out even then from Los Angeles? <u>N.Y. Times</u> architecture critic Paul Goldberger asks of L.A., "Where does it begin? Where does it end?" I think the answers might be Chicago, and Phnom Penh. UIC's Robert Bruegmann writes that the "sprawl" of Southern California is actually more densely populated than eastern cities, and reminds his readers that L.A. was already well dispersed before the automobile culture reached its critical mass. But there is evidently not enough east coast or European candle-power to go up against the simple image of a goddamn palm tree.

And what might the New York or London music scene make of a band like the Germs whose guitarist, Pat Smear, hated "all that boring East coast 'rock critic' rock," preferring Queen, Yes, Bowie, and the Runaways! (I could tell you more about Pat but you'd just understand less and less.) The Germs late singer Darby Crash's lumpen-genius bonafides were as a rule succinctly expressed: "The only people I know around here who are into art are from Phoenix." (Lexicon Devil, *Feral House*)

The Los Angeles music press improved quickly in the eighties. Craig Lee (RIP), who had been in the Bags and managed Redd Kross for a while, soon began to write for the <u>L.A. Weekly</u> and then the <u>Los Angeles Times</u> and he brought an insider, musician's insight to those papers. Metal Mike Saunders did double duty as musician/writer as well. <u>Back Door Man</u> (b. March 1975) was a key fanzine and important writers started there too, notably Phast Phreddie, Don Waller, and Gregg Turner (of the Angry Samoans). <u>No Mag</u> moved from its arty beginnings to fill the music coverage void left by <u>Slash</u>'s demise. <u>Bomp!</u> magazine pre-dated the scene (b. 1969) but got interested in the L.A. bands for awhile too (the Bomp! label re-released the first Last 45, and two great 45s by the San Diego band The Zeros). More sympathetic coverage began coming from others too at the weeklies and dailies (Matt Groening, Chris Morris, Natalie Nichols, Jeff Silberman, Robert Hilburn, Chris Willman, Richard Cromelin, Ken Tucker, Jeff Spurrier, Bruce Duff, Bruce Rhodewalt, Kristine McKenna...). And no other city on the planet had as thorough and long-lived a chronicle of its punk music era as <u>Flipside</u>; their staff seemed to be at every gig from 1977 to 2000 or so.

By the end of 1981 it was already becoming clear we would have a falling out with Unicorn over "Damaged" (and with Laurie over the Meat Puppets). It was nice to be up near Tower Records and the Whisky (though our bands could no longer play there) but we were all glad when Greg and Chuck decided to move the office down to the Redondo Beach space where the electronics stuff was stored. (We actually debated whether to cob the coffee machine from Unicorn; we did and it was the only thing we ever got. It lasted but a few months under our relentless around-the-clock brewage – I might turn in at 11pm to the sound of Henry brewing up another pot or even chewing the grounds as he did the mail.) Mugger now answered the phone, "SST-at-the-beach, how may I help you?" One time I heard him answer, "SST Records, how about a blow?" And then laughing, "Ohh! Sorry Mrs. Ginn! I thought you were D. Boon... Lurch, it's your Mom."

This SST was a one-room office with a shower in the bathroom for a hundred and fifty dollars a month. Unfortunately it was a mile-and-a-half from the beach; I missed the golden age when Black Flag had been able to sleaze by right off the Hermosa strand, with Media Art studio and the Church just a block away. Last year I met Mugger and Holzman and we sat in front of Java Man coffeehouse on Pier Ave. as they told me stories about the Church which once stood two doors north. Java Man itself had been Greg and Medea's house and actually anywhere you pointed was some significant early staging ground (see the aerial Hermosa spread). Holzman remembered working at the Alta-dena drive-thru market still across the street and being intim-idated by the Church punks. He said Greg and Medea came over once when he was wearing a white dress shirt with "DEVO" painted on it; he was going to see them after work. Greg knew that X was opening for Devo and told Holzman to check them out too. Rob admitted to then being uninterested in local bands – too sophisto for that shit.

Here's how Spot explains what Hermosa was:

> "Hermosa Beach was a perfect haven for substantive West Coast bohemia to thrive in the post-WWII era. Surf City's very real legend was the practical as well as the spiritual foundation upon which it built and was allowed to mutate. Perhaps what saved it was the demise of the Red Line streetcars – the Balloon Route being the easiest way for Angelinos to get to the South Bay. Even with the advent of

- Takeyo Kashimura, age 8, Nishikawa dance, Ibaraki Prefecture, 1942.
- Kashimura's 350 yr old Kosho-ji Temple, Totsuka-ku. (Chris Petersen)

•Leroy and Takeyo Petersen, LDS Mission House, Tokyo, Aug. 20, 1957.

•Good old number 3, 3rd base, throws left, swings left.

•9th grade shots of classmates Wayne; Don; Joy; Amy, Crissy... (NP)

•9th grade Naomi at Lawrence Jr. High, Chatsworth.
•Lawrence graduation with dad, June 15, 1979.

•High school girl, 1979 - 1981, Simi Valley. (1,3 by CP)

•Simi Valley High, 1980, from heat-damaged rolls undeveloped until 2006. (NP)

Bela Lugosi

•Birthday card cartoon by Vickie Potts.

the freeway system – which circumvented the area – roads lead tourists and inlanders more easily to Santa Monica and Venice Beach, both towns already noteworthy for their pleasure/amusement piers and beachfronts. Hermosa was a quiet, insular community with a pier only good for fishing and aside from surfing, jazz and intellectualism were not worthy attractions for most people. Another unrecognized salvation may have been the recurring 'energy crises' of the 70s. The locals stayed home more and the unlocals continued staying away. This helped the city resist most development and it remained a unique, unassuming, mostly inexpensive place to live until the late 70s when economic tides finally changed in the carpetbaggers' favors. That's when the Church was approved for commercial replacement and Media Art's lease renewal would jack the rent from $325/mo to $1500/mo. That's when we all made like a Jack Kerouac road trip, split the scene, and we were OUTTA there, Daddy-O!" (S, Jan. 19, 2007)

Spot told an interviewer for Tape Op fanzine how he would awake in his back room at Media Art, walk down to the beach to one of the showers parents use to wash the sand off their kids, strip down, soap up and shower and be ready for that day's recording session. Don't try that today in Hermosa Beach.

But we were in North Redondo now. Spot hung in Hollywood for a while but then followed us down, and Dez moved in with his folks. Dez's dad Ozzie booked the Lighthouse in Hermosa Beach and produced dozens of sessions for Savoy Records (Dez was named for Paul Desmond). Spot's dad was a Tuskegee Airman and he came by once and everyone jumped up to meet him; God knows what he made of his wayward son's menagerie of pals! Mugger was first in line: "Hey everybody, Spot's dad! Hey Spot's dad, I'm Mugger." Mr. Ginn happened by as well and the two WWII flyboys traded war stories at Phelan Avenue SST. Henry slept on the concrete floor for a couple weeks, then moved in with Rosetta. Robo was illegal and had not been allowed back into the country after a December 1981 tour of England. He was replaced short-term by Bill Stevenson of the Descendents; Bill lived with his dad in Hermosa Beach a couple doors from the Ginns. Bill still worked at Jerry's Tackle – Jerry being Keith Morris' dad.

Merrill Ward always had a band going while at Torrance High. He saw Black Flag when his sister's friend Tertia took them to the Polliwog Park gig; he met them later that night at the Church party.

Merrill intended to act and had a style that fit better in a hard rock context. He turned down the Black Flag mic for singing in Overkill whose 45 was recorded by Spot at Music Lab in Silverlake. He worked stages with Mugger and his high-energy creativity is all over the Black Flag radio commercials on the last side of "Everything Went Black." Merrill's doing alright; he's part of an Oregon Satanist sex cult and has a son.

He tells me that one night at the Cathay he was partying with Teresa while Mugger was with Naomi. Naomi drove her car back to SST after the gig and rendezvoused with him in the van. According to Mugger she expected him to stay with her. But that boy was something of a burn-artist as a teenager and he had no such intention. Naomi was apparently drunk enough to get angry with him, but when he disappeared into SST to go to sleep under his desk she could only get into her car and drive home. Hours later the phone rang. Lights were out and I heard Chuck answer quietly, wait, and then tell someone to come over. Naomi shortly came into SST weeping, and bleeding from her wrists. As Chuck led her to the bathroom sink I heard her tell him that her father had called her a tramp and refused to let her into the house. She must have driven back down through L.A., uncertain where to go. When she stopped driving she cut herself, got scared and called, throwing herself again on Black Flag's mercy. Perhaps that seems a counter-intuitive move, but I think it was smart of her.

Chuck was good with her that night, Mugger wouldn't stay with her, so one trauma and two hours later he did, under his desk – a door laid across two short filing cabinets with a piece of heavy carpet nailed across the front – the only private space in the place. Naomi's notes in her calendar for 1982 begin, *"Thought of the month: Lose weight! & Dez Cadena!* • " In the square for July 28, 1982 all she writes is, *"Fear at Cathay. After work see Chuck & Chuck, & Mugger. Get too drunk. Go to SST. <u>Bad night. Chuck D. is a sweetie, helps me!</u>"*

Chuck, Greg, and Spot were the adults and by then had experience with many girls who might be some combination of fragile, damaged, desperate, driven and self-destructive; these girls were often also very intelligent, sensitive and fearless. Here is a representative interior monologue by another such L.A. girl made good-bad, promoter/musician/writer Pleasant Gehman, fretting into her diary at age 17:

> "JANUARY 19, 1977 Life is getting almost unbearable, with my self-manufactured guilt over skipping school, and my terrible fights with Mom.... It's getting really hard to live

with myself and my ways.... If I'm going to be a juvenile delinquent, I wish I would just do it all the way – quit school, live up near the Boulevard, fight a lot, get a notorious rep, etc.... OR, if I'm going to be a 'good girl', do it all the way – honor roll, scholarships, coming home early, a nice relationship with Ma, a boyfriend or two. Instead, all I am is a fuckup, neither here nor there.... I'm just in purgatory, not only in my age and emotions, but in my antics and aspirations as well." (PG, <u>Nuthing Sacred</u>, Sept. 1992)

One night Greg took a call very late and stayed on quite a while, though he did little but listen. When Bill came over the next morning Greg had to explain that he was still sleeping because he was up late on the phone. Bill pried enough details out of him for him to find out that A) Greg got calls in the middle of the night from girls, and B) he didn't. Bill would walk to different spots in the office and try on that idea, "No girls call me in the middle of the night." Mugger's corner, my corner, Chuck's corner... Soon Bill joined Black Flag and then I trust he began to get calls in the middle of the night from girls.

For all Naomi knew, left alone to Los Angeles at 3am, Mugger would answer the phone and hang up on her. Brave girl... The next morning Chuck introduced Naomi to me and told me she had a camera. I had been grousing for months that I couldn't get the new bands photographed. If I remember correctly, Naomi cocked her head slightly and smiled, shook my hand, seemed glad to meet me and thrilled to talk about setting up photo sessions with the bands. The night's trauma seemed out of her mind like a bad dream; she certainly knew I'd heard her come in as my mattress was open to the room. The bandages on her wrists didn't inhibit her. What a girl... (Mugger kept quiet that morning and tells me that Chuck later yelled at him for treating her like that; I also remember Chuck telling me he was sick of Mugger's shit but as I knew very little of what was going on around me he didn't push it.)

Over the next couple days according to Naomi's calendar entries she is back out at gigs (Channel 3, JFA at Whisky; Red Cross at Dancing Waters) mixing with friends, *"Fall off stairs. MDC guy helps! Swollen foot! Bruises on my legs!"*, writing Chuck a thank you note, and four days later on August 1, *"See dad for first time – gives me ugly wallet! Bring mom flowers."*

We didn't keep great house at SST; you could see the battles of natural selection rage over the months as first the cockroaches got the upper hand, then the spiders as they feasted on roach eggs, and then back again. A single drop of Naomi's blood lasted on the bathroom floor for almost a year, until Greg's girlfriend Roseanne stayed the night and offended, went at the whole mess like a Latina tornado.

Naomi solved a major problem for us, as SST was beginning to release records and book gigs for the Minutemen, Saccharine Trust, Saint Vitus, Meat Puppets and others. I could not get the photographers Black Flag counted on (Glen Friedman, Ed Colver) to cover these bands in 1982/3. Mike and D. also set Naomi up to shoot their New Alliance label bands: Descendents, Hüsker Dü, Secret Hate, Tragicomedy, Slovenly, Blood on the Saddle...

Naomi loved it; she used her camera to steady and focus her interest in music and musicians, and earn standing. She made peace with her parents and her father converted their laundry-room into her darkroom. We managed to pay for her film, paper and chemicals.

Naomi's calendar for 1982 is an accelerating blur of action: Gigs, photography, writing bands (TSOL, Damned, Adolescents...) and labels (Dischord, Frontier, Autumn, Touch & Go...), books read (Clockwork Orange, Jack the Ripper), letters sent to Flipside (they were printed), xeroxing lyrics by the Flesheaters or Minor Threat, shooting bands, making prints, attempting to launch a fanzine with Simi friends, interviewing bands, family stuff, boyfriends, partying, moving out of the house, moving back, *"Drive wrong way on F.W.,"* *"Cal. Magazine calls!"* *"See Biscuits and Merrill, fuckheads!"* *"Get invited to No Mag party."* *"Necros & Misfits at Bob's Place. Great Show! Meet Necros, Glen & Doyle!"* *"Bruise city!!!"* *"Call Stacey – I kissed Pete!? Ick!"* *"Jeff Nelson calls! M.T. wants my photos for album cover!"* *"Mr. Miller is a slimy bastard!"* *"Get letter from STABB!"* *"Ed Colver is a jerk!"*, *"Get a job at Benihana's!!! Call the press!!"* *"Fucked day – someone shoots my car."* *"I'sh donsh remesh wha happen! Oh brother,"* bad diet days, good diet days, and her increasing involvement with us at SST (*"Henry is a doll!"* *"Call Joe C. Boring Night!!!"*). Also are irregular notations, three dots – "La Vida Loca" – that appear up to three times a week. They are more carefully inscribed in the day's box early in the year before her activity in the music scene increases, and they don't appear in later years' calendars. They don't seem to line up consistently with references to boys or gigs or parties or drinking sessions but they must mean one or all.

Her paintings were one of the first things she had talked to Dukowski about. Before she was able to get out of Simi Valley and shoot musicians she would shoot slides of bands from photos in the music press, project them onto poster board and then paint high contrast black and white distillations of those half-tones. Most of these were done in 1979-80. Chuck encouraged her, and told her he was fascinated by Frank Gargani's shot of the Minutemen that ran in No Mag and that SST had used as a publicity shot. It's got to be one of the most bizarre choices for a glossy ever – no doubt Duplicate Photo saved one as a joke – their counter was decorated with glossies going back to thirties Hollywood! In the shot D. Boon wears cut-off jeans and Chuck thought the long white threads hanging from his shorts called to mind the scraggly hair hanging from the balls of a bull. So he asked Naomi to make a larger-than-life painting of just D. It was an imposing two piece painting eight foot tall! Naomi did this painting before ever meeting D. When she does in April 1982 she notes, "*See Chuck and Greg – Meet D. Boon, Short guy!*"

Mugger was still growing up; he was a sixth grade drop-out who lived on the beach or circulated thru the Hollywood punk crashpads until he ran across Black Flag and impressed Greg with his capacity for work and organization. He would refer to Greg as his father as he hadn't had one. Henry writes, "If you ever made a (complaining) noise about anything, Mugger would just start laughing and say something like, 'This isn't Van Halen! Get it happening!'" (Get in the Van) Mugger was famous for many things. The first young kids who climbed up on stage just stood there dumbfounded at the novel perspective. Mugger and his string of seconds began to force them back into the crowd and this game evolved quickly into stage-diving. He was voted runner-up "Asshole of the Year" by the readers of Flipside for his work assisting these stage-divers reach the proper velocity (I imagine he garnered a preponderance of the female vote too – Jerry Roach won the honor). I remember the day Mugger turned 18; he bemoaned the fact that he would now be risking statutory rape charges on a routine basis. Mugger was our paymaster and thereafter treated Naomi with respect, though the natural voltage of her personality did seem to dip around him. In her address book, which her brother Chris let me look through, she editorialized after only one name, Mugger's. Just the word "Fascismo," one of the old SST buzzwords, generally used as a begrudging compliment – coined by Mugger or maybe Chuck Biscuits, derived from the Dukowski maxim, "Anarchy for me, Fascism for you."

5. Rec-Biz

When SST moved back to the south bay from West Hollywood, I inevitably stumbled into the printers, typesetters, and photo-labs in the Torrance/Gardena area that Greg and Chuck had taken stuff to a year earlier. They worried that these places had been among the businesses that narc-ed them out to the cops. For a short bit after the Phelan Ave./Redondo office, SST was in the garage behind Greg's sister Linda's house in Redondo. Her husband John had the original Black Flag van, a '64 Econoline, and he told me that he was pulled over by the Hermosa or Torrance cops whenever he drove it. But the only problem I encountered was cleaning up a couple unpaid bills caused by the Torrance eviction. These mom and pop businesses by and large loved us and our crazy shit. They all read the papers and saw on TV what a menace Black Flag was... But they had liked Greg, Chuck, Mugger, Spot, Raymond, Mike and D. and they seemed to like me.

  The first Black Flag sleeve and early flyers were done at a printer in South Central run by a Puerto Rican family. Son John Macias worked for his dad there, saw a flyer and decided to check out a gig and became one of the more forbidding characters of the early eighties as lead singer of Circle One, and all-purpose pit-monitor. I was glad I'd shaken his hand at the printer's, because you did not want to be some unknown hippie when John turned back to the stage and from inside the pit glared at the crowd looking for trouble. His father wouldn't print an insert for the Dicks album because it had a drawing of a dick on it. John was also a Christian, he would charge the door at punk gigs and the security jocks would all run to stop him, while his disciples would then break through into the hall for free. Ten years later John was preaching on the Santa Monica pier when the cops interrupted him. You don't interrupt John Macias when he's preaching the word of God! He faced them down unarmed and was shot to death. Sainthood will be slow train a'comin' for an L.A. punk.

  Spot found that one of the owners of Media Art – the studio where the first SST and early Posh-Boy and Dangerhouse releases were recorded – had opened a new studio in Redondo Beach. Total Access made it possible for us to record bands on credit, get the records out, get paid and then pay them at 120 days. John Golden at K-Disc Mastering was another great asset; each session to cut lacquers for new releases came complete with a further good-humored lesson in the technical history of the recording arts and he rarely put us on the clock even on projects whose final assemblage went on there. To their amazement, no doubt, Wyn Davis at Total Access and John Golden at K-Disc found their flexibility with SST repaid years later as new bands and labels sought them out for that very connection to us. I was back at Total Access in early 2006 for the first time since 1985 to work on Unknown Instructors releases. Wyn was in Hawaii getting married but there on the lobby wall were framed Hüsker Dü, Descendents, and Black Flag album covers. Above them were large platinum record/cassette/CD plaques for Sublime, No Doubt, and Guns 'n Roses... Vodicka remembers taking a New Alliance project up to K-Disc the Monday after Nirvana appeared on Saturday Night Live (Jan. 11, 1992) and John told him he stayed up with one of his sons to watch. "His response was something like, 'I don't see what the big deal is; Black Flag blows this away.'" John was/is the sweetest, straightest family man you could imagine, and he liked us and rooted for us.

We'd run our cut lacquers down to James G. Lee Processing because they were nearby in Gardena where a lot of the industry had its stampers made. The Lee family liked to give you a tour the first time you came in. Watching them run the lacquers thru the nickel-plating bath impressed one that any music could survive the shit it took to press vinyl. If I remember, that nickel father made a number of mothers from which stampers were made, each of which might press two thousand LPs. The American standard in the platinum era was to run LPs until the stamper broke, run stampers til the mother broke and run mothers until the father broke, which is why audiophiles gladly paid more for UK, German, or Japanese pressings. That wasn't our problem.

SST found the Virco pressing plant in Alhambra via Joe Nolte of the Last. They'd released their first 45 in November 1977 on their own Backlash label. And through SST, Virco was soon cranking on New Alliance, Slash-Ruby, Frontier, Posh-Boy, and Unicorn label catalog. Virginia Watts ran it with her husband and we got to know this elderly couple well. Mike Watt took special interest in the mechanical aspects of what they did there and heard sixties Nashville lore from their pressman, Hank.

We printed covers at Stoughton Printing in City of Industry. Mike dealt with owner Jack Stoughton, another WWII vet, and every time Mike reordered the Hüsker Dü "Land Speed Record" covers with the photos of be-medalled, flag-draped coffins, Jack would give Mike a little lecture about the boys who didn't come home. I worked with Jack's son, Ace, and considered myself lucky to not have to try to explain Pettibon artwork to Jack. Ace made mild objection to a song-title on the Sluts album ("Mom's Cunt") but he knew it wasn't an SST release *per se*; we were just helping out some pals (Dave Slut's band got to be great but before we could record them for a second album they got home to New Orleans and fell apart, hocking instruments for heroin we heard). Still I sent the Nig-Heist album cover over to the more corporate Modern Printing out of consideration for the Stoughton family. (The cover was Spot's idea: Chatty Cathy going down on Knucklehead while he pulls her string, perfectly drawn by Kurt Markham's girlfriend Nancy Maurer.)

Ten years earlier Virco had been pressing Yazoo, gospel, glee club records and the last of the hippie independent labels; now they were choking the chain stores with local punk rock vinyl. Rodney Bingenheimer was playing a lot of local bands on KROQ and other DJs there were picking up on them too, and over at KPFK Richard Meltzer was hosting a weekly late night bacchanal of records, blasphemy and live music – he was soon fired by the Pacifica "radicals," and replaced by Andrea 'Enthal who had covered music for the dying L.A. Free Press, I think. We'd go up to Virco with a crew of people to sticker over MCA logos on 25,000 "Damaged" albums covers, or stuff 15,000 Pettibon posters and stickers into "Everything Went Black" covers to save 3¢ per (the crew would be bits of BF, Minutemen, SST, and maybe friends like Stella of KXLU and Carmel of No Mag/Faulty). Then Unicorn was granted one injunction after another and we couldn't sell the records or pay our bills. I was on the witness stand at the L.A. County Courthouse when the judge was handed exhibit A, the "Everything Went Black" album cover with Black Flag's name excised but Pettibon's garden shears waving menacingly; judgey did not like the looks of that drawing! Greg and Chuck spent five days in jail. Bill Stevenson told Jay Babcock, "I didn't visit them in jail. I was just at the law office, trying to prepare this writ of habeas corpus to get 'em out of there." Henry is quoted by Michael Azerrad as saying that Greg's first words on his release were, "Practice is at seven." (Our Band Could Be Your

Life, *Little, Brown*)

Unicorn wasn't paying Virco, nor just about anyone else. Greg paid to sublet the offices from Unicorn when Unicorn was not paying its own rent. But Virco, even as they lost the Slash account to Warners, refused to settle with Unicorn and incurred its own legal bills as a way of aiding us. Walter Hurst and Max Abrams were Black Flag's lawyers; they went out of their way to keep the bill down but that meant Greg, Chuck, and Bill had loads of case history reading to do. Greg explained to Jay Babcock,

> "Every day we'd take the bus from Redondo out to Hollywood and Vine, where he was, and work on it. We did a lot of legal filing, wrote a lot of the motions, did a lot of research. We didn't end up paying him completely until years after the band broke up. He was so good to us." (GG, L.A. Weekly, June 22, 2001)

Walter had published a line of books that attempted to demystify the music business for musicians. Greg and Chuck had managed to spare Mugger and me any liability but we did feel additional pressure to make the label happen; Max would call me every month or two to ask how business was. Thank God it was improving. What had happened in L.A. in 1980-81 was beginning to happen out and around the rest of the country. The European embargo seemed to last until 1987; they missed most of the best records and bands.

Greg explained to me Unicorn's corporate shell game, which became clearer when its label declared Chapter 11 bankruptcy to fend off Virco and others. He had me check the distributors we shared with Unicorn and sure enough Anne at Rough Trade found that Unicorn had deposited an RT check to the bankrupt label into a different, still viable corporate account – fraudulent use of bankruptcy laws, court-ordered conversion to Chapter 7, game over... Chuck told Jay,

> "You know, we barely stayed alive. All of these people in this teeny space... It didn't take long before it started tearing at the seams of things. Too many people, too little food, too little sleep – it fucked everybody up." (CD, *Ibid.*)

By the time Black Flag was free of Unicorn, Virco had lost Hank back to Nashville and were only brokering jobs out to other plants. Those plants would come to us and try to cut Virco out, but I ran the Minutemen and Hüsker Dü double albums, Black Flag "Slip It In," and some other new titles through them anyway; we owed them more than money. Mike Watt and Greg understood but Mugger was pushing to save us the money by going elsewhere. We were going to be paying off legal bills for the next decade and though we could now sell Black Flag records and pay Virco, we couldn't save them. We suddenly needed a plant that could run cassettes as well, and CDs were already being talked about. Several generations of record industry mom and pops were dying. But it had been to me that Virginia made her final sales pitch: "You know we love you up here." Those old girls, they don't fight fair.

6. Nikon Eye

Our young girl, meanwhile, had wiped our photographer problem clean off the table. Lest one imagine this was easy for her, here's Alison Braun, a.k.a., Mouse, another prominent girl-photog of the period:

> "I have trouble because bands don't take themselves seriously and I gave up trying... But like the Minutemen and Saccharine Trust, they're just always scattered unless they're at practice like at SST. I can never get them all at one time. At their gigs they're always floating around with their friends. It's just hard, very hard..." (AB, No Mag, 1982)

Alison tells me she was too young to drive at the time of this No Mag profile so her father dropped her off at El Coyote to meet Bruce Kalberg. I asked her, What was your dad thinking?! She responded, "My dad was a good sport. He knew he couldn't stop me from being a punk, so he sort of became incorporated into it.... He struck up unlikely friendships with Lucky Lehrer, Biafra, and El Duce." (March 16, 2007)

Naomi shot Saccharine Trust at practice; she shot Saint Vitus under the power lines behind SST in Redondo; she shot our bands at gigs, recording sessions, and at SST. She also shot touring bands: Minor Threat, Bad Brains, Butthole Surfers, Misfits, Necros, Big Boys, Dicks.... She ran through a Redondo Beach cemetery with Saint Vitus, quickly shooting set-ups to stay ahead of the groundskeepers. Concerned citizens reported four drunken hippies sprawled out front of the Thirsty Club in Redondo (see "Thirsty and Miserable" EP cover) and Naomi had to sweet-talk the responding officers. Saint Vitus might have had trouble on their own convincing the cops they weren't actual derelicts. And she shot an insane session with Mugger's band, the Nig-Heist, backstage at the Cathay de Grande. Merrill wore gold body-paint and a g-string, and the band was caught in what I think the professionals term "water-sports" – as you look those pics over you can all but hear Naomi's laughter egging them on.

As promotional photos from record companies are often run uncredited, I tried to push publications to credit her, as compensation for how little we could pay her. It irked me then and it still does that I regularly forgot to. When her restaurant job allowed, she would come down with her contact sheets and prints and we'd decide what to run copies of. I think her best early stuff was the Saint Vitus stuff. She met them at SST in Redondo and shot them against the wall and out under the power lines – both excellent portraits. I probably gave her a tape of their rough mixes and talked to her about trying to emphasize their psychedelic aspects rather than the metal ones. She nodded and suggested using infra-red film. She did that next time then in the cemetery and it was perfect. I was impressed. So was everybody else. Chuck had Naomi shoot Suzi Gardner as Eve-with-apple out at Spahn Ranch amid startled hunters staked out in the bush, and though the snake on Suzi's shoulders is virtually invisible in the infrared image, it made a striking cover for Würm's "Feast." She'd come in to SST usually on a Sunday when things were quiet and show me stuff she'd taken. The shots she'd made prints of were the best by her lights and I and whoever else was there would laugh and respond, "Wow! Great!" to these images of the geek-schmucks we knew as SST recording artists. She'd softly breathe out, "Thanks."

Her brother Chris said she was very proud of what she thought was her first iconic image – a two-shot composition of Ian and Henry outside of Unicorn-Santa Monica (July 13, 1982, Get in the Van, 2nd ed., pg. 66). Another shot from that session is nearby (Minor Threat w/ Henry, Robo). It's significant that Naomi valued these shots that show the two D.C. buds letting her in on their relationship. (top photo: Henry tossing his 13-ball into the air while Ian, just slightly behind Henry, holds his hands in front looking flatly at the camera; bottom photo: Ian has turned and is flipping Henry off behind his back and grinning like psycho DeNiro.) I remember Greg looking at the composite and being convinced that Naomi had revealed the real Ian, or at least what Ian really thought of Henry leaving Washington to join Black Flag. (It's often forgotten that Henry helped start the Dischord label with Ian and Jeff.) I didn't have an opinion on that, but then I knew I wasn't up to speed in terms of paranoia. But I thought it was a good sign if Greg was conscious of the price Henry might be paying for having joined Black Flag.

More importantly: *What a joy Naomi was to work with!* I packed away my camera, and never called Glen or Ed again.

Naomi became another extra-Black Flag SST character a la Pettibon, Medea, Spot, Mugger, Davo, Jordan and others. One minute she was being stood up by Simi or Oxnard bands she wanted to shoot and interview for a fanzine that nobody else seemed to lift a finger to make a reality, and the next she was SST's house photographer. We were the best people money could buy, but there was no money. We were all nuts enough to be doing it for art and action. We required more involvement than any mere job could provide. Greg and Black Flag's stature made this an easy, obvious choice – for the guys anyway – and though Greg was not a romantic we did our best to run on loyalty, although in Los Angeles loyalty, like friendship, family, and love seemed somehow altered.... But if the world didn't know it yet, we at SST knew that there was nothing occurring anywhere else in music that was more important than what we were doing – not out of New York or London, not at independent labels and certainly not at the majors. Whenever Spot came out of the studio with some new, amazing recordings it sent a jolt of confirming, inspiring energy back through every other band in our orbit; it was all lifting towards... a critical mass of something or other.

We didn't consider our bands punk. SST would get calls from casting agents looking for punk extras and Greg would laugh and tell them we didn't know any punk rockers, though Merrill could be counted on to dye his hair blue and go do a "CHiPs" or "Quincy" episode (he is also notable in the Tom Petty video, "Free Fallin'" as one of the vampires). We first presented Saint Vitus to Black Flag's draw at Dancing Waters, San Pedro (Aug. 6, 1982). The crowd was grumbling plenty when they saw these long-hairs setting up on stage. Henry went up to soften the blow, "I know you guys aren't into slow songs..." It worked; Saint Vitus weren't torn limb from limb. They opened with "Burial at Sea"; that helped! We saw a lot of great bands, but what the world considered punk or hardcore we paid little attention to. Once KROQ went synth-wave in 1982 the radio at SST was tuned to the hard rock stations (KMET, KLOS), the country stations (KLAC, KFOX) the black stations (KDAY, KACE), or the tin pan alley station (KPRZ). On Tuesday night Stella was on; Saturday am KLON played blues; in the pm KFOX played Guatemalan music. (We had no real record player at SST until 1984; Spot would use his need to check test pressings as an opportunity to invite himself over to various girls' houses.)

Naomi, like the rest of us, didn't simply run to the brightest spotlight. She seemed to build her strongest friendships with the black sheep, Saccharine Trust and Saint Vitus; I believe they were her first assigned shoots for us in August 1982, although her calendar shows her returning to SST to shoot Henry and Mugger within a week of her *bad night*. Spot bonded with her as they used the same Nikon – the FTN Photomic, of which Spot says, "Great fuckin' cameras and built like tanks; you could kill somebody with one in a fight if you had to." (Spot shot Black Flag from their days as Panic in 1978, when indeed many a gig might force one to consider one's defensive options.) Naomi was given her camera by her mother's brother, Toshio, who Chris writes was a lover of art, photography and anything American; he also loved to laugh, and followed his father as priest/sojo at the Kosho-ji temple. Heft aside, a camera was intrinsically a pretty good defensive weapon for a girl out on the town. Jennifer Precious Finch, years before L7, was a young photographer (see her nearby shot of John Macias):

> "Being a 14-year-old girl made me kind of invisible. I don't think anyone was even paying attention when I had my camera…. It was just something I enjoyed, and it allowed me access." (JPF, L.A. Weekly, Nov. 3, 2006)

When Spot saw that Naomi had talent and was serious he gave her his tripod (on Nov. 12, 1982 by her calendar). He writes that she went from having little to distinguish herself from the other girls floating around the scene to being fully accepted as one of us very quickly.

Naomi worked closely with Henry on a series of portraits that made concrete images out of changes he was making in his life/art. (My favorite shot of Henry is in the Portfolio section; he tells me this was the one session that Naomi actively coached him – she wanted to see him project *power*.) She practically specialized in shots where you can see the easy laughter going on between artist and subject. She was an insider and got casual, candid shots of the great musicians of the day. She was catalyst as well – nothing like the presence of a fun, good-looking girl to make a band forget how much they hate each other and remember why they love being in a band. These weren't the shots we could often use for PR purposes but they constitute an important aspect of her work.

Henry put together an amazing batch of photos from all comers for his book, Get in the Van. Naomi's 25 range from fierce, full-band portraits of Black Flag live in Richmond or Torrance, to the post-performance glow of October Faction (the model for Joe Baiza's cover drawing on their first album), to horseplay for Naomi by Minor Threat, by Ian and Henry, by Henry and Nick Cave, and a striking shot of Henry and Chuck wherein Chuck – Henry's true sponsor in the band until Greg's traumatic, year-long, slo-mo firing of him – looks happy again one year on. (When the Unicorn legal battle put Black Flag on ice for 1983 Chuck reunited his old band, Würm, and began a new band Swa with Ted Falconi of Flipper and Merrill on vocals. As Gremsky had no band to book he returned to Poland to work for Solidarnosc.) To Naomi these horseplay shots were not taken for me or the media; they were taken as if for some mutant family album, her own documentation that these were her friends.

I gave her the fool's errand of trying for full-band live shots, which, aside from composition and lighting questions (always problems in the dumps our bands played), are near impossible to grab. Finding that moment and perspective when all players have eyes open and non-dork expressions on their faces and no mic booms or guitar necks or stage-divers or security obscuring them, and no hangers-on lined up behind their amps looking bored is virtually impossible. On page 73 of Get in the Van (2nd ed.) you can see this problem in Naomi's shot of Black Flag at the Ukrainian Hall (Dec. 10, 1982). Hard to mess with D. Boon if he wants to stand behind Greg's amp, but there's also Laura (Rapunzel), Kim Pilkington (RIP) and at least six others and that's just stage right. This was a massive gig, one of Biscuits' last, and they played the heavy shit for hours until they just wore... the... pit... **down**. I remember setting Naomi up on the sidewall where she could get up on a chair and frame the stage with a telephoto lens. Friedman wisely shot the soundcheck! In Black Flag's case you could do that. (see James Parker's Rollins bio, Turned On, *Cooper Square*, for Thurston's description of a BF soundcheck spied thru a window – May 31, 1982, Long Island.) After the Ukrainian Hall gig, I explained the problem to the band and Mugger and Davo (and D. Boon!); Naomi next set up in a small balcony at Mi Casita in Torrance (Jan. 14, 1983) and we kept the stage clear. Here it was stage lighting that was insufficient and no room at all for backlights or hangers-on. You can see the result on pg. 78 of Get in the Van; it's a B-roll shot and not the better one that we used for press.

While concentrating through the viewfinder a photographer at these gigs might also easily find herself landed on by some airborne punk; indeed in more than one picture of Naomi one can see bruises and scratches all over her ankles. There are a number of accidental exposures of club ceilings that seem caused by being hit from behind, and one amazing color shot where the band (Life Sentence, I think) is framed by bodies closing in from the sides and one dropping from above. Mouse tells me she was knocked unconscious at one gig when Milo of the Descendents landed on her. Bruce Connor tells Greil Marcus regarding his late seventies photography of the early SF punk bands at the Mab,

> "I had always liked the idea of action photos, like – sports events.... Or *combat* photography. I always thought, gosh, combat photography. Maybe I could work on that here."
> (BC, Aperture, Summer 2006)

Naomi saw such combat, plus that L.A. factor – some bit of extra alienation and animal charge to the tumult.

The live choreography that rock and roll bands had settled into by the mid-seventies was designed for arenas. It all got rote when FM got formatted and the business got serious about platinum. Films conceived and shot in the cultural revolution phase of the late sixties went unreleased for decades: "The Rock and Roll Circus," "Festival Express," "Cocksucker Blues." That's how quick it changed. In the wake of Altamont, Manson, etc., bands like the Beatles, Rolling Stones, Led Zeppelin began to ask themselves why bother trying to help other bands with their labels or film projects. Chuck saw the Who in 1982 at the L.A. Coliseum (he went as a lark with Kelley and Rick) and I remember him being amazed at how boring it had been, given that the audience was huge. Even the dim cheer that went up when Townsend did his windmill guitar strokes just emphasized how deathly the whole deal was. The Clash opened and were being handed an extinguished torch. Chuck says they all went from the Coliseum to the Anti-Club to see the Minutemen! I once dragooned Mike Watt to the L.A. Forum to see Rush with Kelley and Rick, and Mike picked up immediately on how their total sound structure changed as they went into their mid-set "2112" section – suddenly they were not a Police-damaged AOR band but a seventies prog acid-rock band again. I remember Geddy Lee jumping around like Peter Pan. The Who and Rush were older bands and had earned their own stylistic dementias; younger post-Van Halen bands wore white Reebok's, feathered hair and the players would gesture in synchronized rocking motions with big shit-eating grins on their faces. That was the Music Professional circa 1980, essentially co-opting the few approved photographers into pre-paid hagiographers. The punk reaction – a naturalistic clutz-cool – both challenged and freed photographers.

    Photographer and Group f/64 member Edward Weston thought photography was intrinsically an honest medium and "so the photographer is much more likely to approach nature in the spirit of inquiry, of communion, instead of the saucy swagger of self-dubbed 'artists'." MoMA's John Szarkowski wrote in 1990 that photographers "relationship between their work and their lives has become casual and improvisatory." Susan Sontag wrote that "death haunts all photographs of people," and that Americans being "less convinced of the permanence of any basic social arrangements" than Europeans, came to the camera with "partisan" designs. (On Photography, *Picador*) Roland Barthes thought photographs actual "agents of Death." Photography critic John Berger considered them to be in "opposition to history." The best known rock photographer, Annie Leibovitz, is rather a hagiographer, now well into her baroque phase at <u>Vanity Fair</u>, though that work is a consistent extension of her work at <u>Rolling Stone</u>. She shoulda shot more bar gigs! And PBS's "American Masters" on her was unconvincing in its treatment of her. It fully imploded when the master herself says of the power her editors give to her celeb subjects, "I think the famous people are winning."

    For punk-era music photographers truth, partisanship, and death won out. The work is indeed in partisan, personal opposition to the fake history laid out by courtiers to the platinum throne. Glen Friedman may be best known as a music photographer but his most important work was of the early DogTown Z-boys as they invented non-linear skateboarding in empty swimming pools. Ed Colver's best shot must be the close-up of Ian MacKaye cradled in the crowd (pg. 44-5, Blight at the End of the Funnel), three of whose faces are subject as well; you might also want to check out his photo-spreads of the LAPD attending gigs and even the 1980 premiere of "The Decline of Western Civilization" at the Hollywood Theater! At the Black Flag reunion gig at the Santa Monica Civic Don Lewis found a religious vibe in his shots, including one of Henry in the crowd looking up into the light with eyes closed and mouth open slightly; the audience around him are in deep shadows but someone's hand is poised over his head as if to anoint him or finger Him to the Romans. Jenny Lens writes, "I didn't even look at 95% of what I shot 'til recently," and given she shot the early Hollywood bands up until 1980 and so many of them died young, one imagines her communing with the dead in her darkroom.

    Nihonjinron is the theory of Japanese exceptionalism. The latest example of it is a book by Masahiko Fujiwara. In the Financial Times (March 10/11, 2007) he notes the Japanese preference for the cherry blossom representing *mononoaware*, "the pathos of the fleeting moment," and contrasts that with the occident's preference for the sturdier rose. The Asia Times columnist, Spengler, builds on this,

> "It is beautiful to view cherry blossoms; in a way, it is even more beautiful to view the Japanese as they sit under the blooming cherry trees, for their unique affinity to nature's moments of beauty constitutes one of humankind's most exquisite protests against mortality."
> (atimes.com, Apr. 3, 2007)

Spengler also calls the Japanese penchant for taking photographs as another of these protests. I wish Naomi had taken photographs like that, but she just wasn't that Japanese I guess. There would surely be a better record of the various SSTs and people of the scene. We were all music focused; we weren't that conscious of documenting as we did. Raymond gave up trying to convince Black Flag they should file away a few copies of each flyer for posterity; the extras were used as scrap paper or to write the mailing list on, or to correspond with fans. Naomi only shot me when a trade magazine asked for a photo. I'm glad one did, it's nice to have them.

Seeing Naomi's work now, I see she found more clean full-band live moments than I appreciated then, though many of her best live shots are Naomi on her own framing action portraits of Joe Baiza, or Dave Chandler, or Dez Cadena, or Steve McDonald, or Curt Kirkwood, D. Boon, Henry Rollins, Greg Ginn...

It was asking for trouble if I sent out shots of any single member of a band because SST bands were *bands*. Chuck and I were into what Henry was accomplishing in Hollywood with his spoken word, and with his written word in the Village Voice and Spin and set Naomi after solo shots of Henry. Greg didn't seem so enthusiastic. Derrick Bostrom sent me a cassette of excellent minimalist, slack rockabilly he wrote, sang and played during Meat Puppets downtime in 1984, and I was ready to go right to work releasing it – it had a sound as if Lou Reed had recorded for Monument. But Derrick immediately halted it when he got the no-go vibe from the Kirkwoods (this, even though they were always attempting to replace him). And see the Saccharine Trust flyers I repro'ed in R&TPN, and similarly the Minutemen, Hüsker Dü, the Descendents, Overkill, the Stains.... I think Saint Vitus liked each other the most. So though we generally could not use them, Naomi took wonderful solo portraits; she'd make prints and give them to the musicians. However deeply she was into photography itself and working for SST, it was always about her favorite musicians in her favorite bands.

Jack Brewer of Saccharine Trust writes of Naomi:

> "We hung out for a short while in the early days. But she was on to me. And knew me too well to fall for my saccharine lines. She had class. She loved the music and was very supportive of those who worked at making the music.... As she documented it I think she put a lot of faith and trust into the musician. Perhaps saw them as noble. But she held herself up throughout. I hope no one hurt her."
> (JB, May 7, 2005)

I expect she did get hurt here and there, it was that kind of time and place, but Naomi had unusual expectations, if they even warrant the word. And SST was worth it, and a relatively safe place to be. Elsewhere in the L.A. music world the drugs and alcohol and sex and egos often ruled the art and so the art might not be worth the bother of the crappy clubs, the bad PAs, the drunk assholes, the incomprehension, the pedophiles and Los Angeles' endless supply of sad, lost girls, and angry, restless boys. There was a steady stream of quite young people in those years dropping dead from drugs, and then suddenly from Aids as well. They'd be excitable kids loving music one year, then suddenly be seen looking like zombies, then they'd stop coming, then you'd hear they were dead. Pettibon has a drawing of a girl on the street with a syringe that reads, "So far away from my record collection" (see R&TPN, pg. 432). Paul Beahm/Bobby Pyn/Darby Crash, casualty-to-be perhaps summed it up best in his masterful conflation of religion and science in the Germs' tune, Manimal: *"Evolution is a process too slow to save my soul."*

2
JUNE 1977

RADIO FREE HOLLYWOOD

POP! BEST BURGER IN TOWN

MOTELS: BEHIND THE BREAK

THE DOGS! STILL UNDERGROUND

MORE!!

RUNAWAYS! **BLONDIE!**

*I picked this up at Peaches Records across the street from the Vogue Theater where I worked.

NEO BOYS in concert SATURDAY MAY 26th
NORTHWEST ARTISTS WORKSHOP 117 NW 5th
8 & 10 PM $1.00 all ages

```
KYM         VOCALS
JENNIFER    GUITAR
KT          BASS
PAT         DRUMS
```

Neo Boys was regularly booked at Revenge Club and the New Arts Center. Since the demise of these two underage halls, the band has avoided the bar circuit with the belief that concerts should be open to a wide audience of all ages.

Neo Boys supports the California-type liquor law, a more lenient view toward minors.

```
JUN 3, 1978    LEWIS & CLARK COLLEGE    FIRST LIVE PERFORMANCE
JUL 2, 1978    EARTH TAVERN             OPENED FOR NY BAND, TELEVISION
AUG 27, 1978   PORTLAND STATE UNIV      OPENED FOR LA BAND, ZEROS
MAR 16, 1979   LONG GOODBYE             HEADLINED HOUSE SOLD OUT TO 250
```

•Neo Boys pr, Portland, 1979.

T16   NIGHEIST

"Snort My Load"

Ah, the follow up to the oft-slagged conceptual B-sided "Walkin Down the Street" 45 in no less than LP form. Released in conjunction with the third or maybe fourth but certainly last ever national/european tour. Ashes of progressive thought still smoldering metaphorically.

Highlighted by the joyful romping "Tight Little Pussy" and incredibly insightful "Big Wheels" and including the pinnacle of modern realist thinking, "Life in General "Snort My Load" continues from which point the American Men's Room stall wall leaves off and takes us/you in the' direction of

ONOMATOPOEIA BEFORE MUSIC
Education & Entertainment   ONO is: Ric, P. Michael, travis
ONO, P.O. Box 702, Wilmette, IL 60091

© ONO 1983

•When Systematic wound down Optional Music, UCB MFA KALX DJ Jon Boshard and I commenced Thermidor and the rest is almost history.

GENETICS

A PERIODICAL RECORD OF INVESTIGATIONS BEARING ON HEREDITY AND VARIATION

Published by the Genetics Society of America

EDITORIAL OFFICE: MONTEREY HALL/ROOM 332, CALIFORNIA STATE UNIVERSITY, NORTHRIDGE
NORTHRIDGE, CALIFORNIA 91330   TELEPHONE: (213) 885-2069

Dear Joe-

Just got your call--had to write further about Meat Puppets--

You'd be really smart to do a 45 for them--I'm SURE with the right publicity it would do really well among the punk crowd. They could probably record it in 4 or 8 track really cheap.

It's rea-ly difficult to describe them--they're ten times faster than any other band around--they make the Urinals sound like old grannys! But amid all the cacophany there is definite structure--with a guitar that sounds as if its been unleashed from another planet. I know that sounds like preposterous hype but no kidding, Kurt is the most demented, innovative guitarist I've heard--somehow he combines total cacophany and noise with offhand, almost accidental-sounding riffs that are so funny and unpredictable-- He is a true original, in a world in which there are dangerously few of them. One of my favorites of theirs is a cover version of "Sugar Mountain." There's a slight, perversely country flair to some of their songs, but it all goes by so fast you're never really sure what happened at all. And on top of the pounding haelstrom, there's Kurt or Kris' singing--both are similarly inflamed, wailing and whining so hard it looks like their veins are going to explode. Live, they are the most exciting <u>and</u> funny band I've seen in <u>years</u>--maybe EVER. It's not "kooky" humor--its just that they do things that sound so unpredictable that you have to laugh.
There's only three of them--bass, drums and guitar, and the bass and guitarist are brothers. I think they're all under 21, and very cute too. They look like real nerds; the authentic kind you'd find wandering aimlessly around some computer science department ....and then they get up on stage and explode. It's so funny...

Well, I guess that's it. Whenever I think about Meat Puppets I go on and on...EVERYONE here who has seen them is crazy about them...
I'll write them and tell them to send you a tape. I don't know if they have any that are truly reprsentative of their live sound, but maybe they can get working on one.

I'll have Ed call you soon.(He doesn't have a phone.)

Oh--If YOU guys are intersted in re-releasing the Monitor 45 let us know because I'd rather have you do it than someone else.
See you, Laurie

*Laurie re the Meat Puppets 1981; I was still at Systematic in Berkeley, she was editing the CSUN journal.

Hermosa Beach, California, 1947

1. The Lighthouse b.1950.

2. The Insomniac, 1958-1963.

3. Either/Or Bookstore.

4. The Sea Sprite motel.

5. Burbage Theatre, early 70s / Media Art Studio 1975-1981 upstairs, including Spot's backroom apt.

6. Original Media Art location.

7. Cove Theater / Easy Reader offices upstairs.

8. Baptist church / The Colony / The Church.

9. Greg & Medea's house / Java Man Coffee.

10. SST Electronics - proto Global Booking / Pier Music.

11. Hermosa Bathhouse / The Würmhole.

•Spot's annotations:
"The Sea Sprite was the dive where most jazz greats and rock sleazeballs stayed while in Hermosa. I interviewed Mose Allison here for the Easy Reader."
"The Garden of Eden, vegetarian restaurant where I worked and first started talking to Greg about music"
"The Surf Hut was an essential Hermosa eatery, where old guard surfdogs and low end riff-raff congregated, and the cooks knew about punk rock."
"Sven Holmes ran the Fleetwood in Redondo and was the first person I ever heard talk about The

"Surf City, U.S.A."

12. Sven Holmes apartment.

13. Wild Wheels.

14. El Yaqui / Los Muchachos restaurant.

15. Garden of Eden.

16. Liz's Café.

17. Surf Hut Café.

Just outside the photo in varied directions were Ozzie Cadena's junkshop, Dave Ratman Levine's apt., the Holzmans' house, and within 1 mile were the Moose Lodge, the Fleetwood, Jerry's Tackle, the Ginns' house, the Stevensons' house, and within 2 miles the Navettas' house, Polliwog Park, SST-Redondo, Global 1, Total Access Studio, the Bel Air/Revelaire Club, Tom's Thirsty Club...

nones."

e Either/Or Bookstore was the last visible bastion of the old 1950s/60s bohemian gestalt that took t there alongside the surf culture. It effectively became the Superego of Hermosa."

e Insomniac... legendary beat-era coffeehouse with live music/poetry, etc. from 1958-63, an ortant link in the whole west coast bohemian/hot rod/surf/biker/cool culture."

•Panic. Photos sent to Bomp! on Oct. 5, 1978: in Redondo Beach, and at their North Redondo practice-pad on Aviation Blvd at Grant.

•Jan. 27, 1979, first gig as Black Flag, drawing by Raymond Pettibon. (courtesy ratsound.com)

•SSTs Torrance..., Redondo..., Hawthorne..., Global 1-Redondo...

Lawndale…, Global 2-Torrance…, Long Beach 1 (Chris Collins)…, Long Beach-2. (all JC, except noted)

•A spectre haunts neo-Hermosa, Dec. 2006. (JC)
•Black Flag and Medea shot by Chris D. in West L.A., Dec. 1979. (Spot)

•Medea, the Church, Hermosa Beach, early 1980, Spot had written "The brains behind it all" on the back. (S)

Easy Reader

Volume XI, Number 44   REFLECTIONS FROM THE SOUTH BAY   FREE /   June 25, 1981

CLOCKWORK BLACK

"If you ever come back to Hermosa, we'll put you in the hospital, and then you can recuperate in jail"

BY CHRIS WILLMAN

Alvin Toffler would probably be interested in Black Flag. The hardcore punk band's music seems to validate his Future Shock hypothesis, which states that the world is accelerating at such a rapid pace, people are unable to keep up with it. Like modern technology, Black Flag doesn't waste time waiting for anyone. Their songs are often under a minute in length, almost never over two minutes, and have no time for wasted sentiments or self indulgent guitar solos. If there are a few cuts and gashes along the way, well, it's all for the greater good.

The pace of songs like "No Values" and "You Bet We've Got Something Personal Against You" makes disco's 180-beats-a-minute and even most other punk bands seem slow by comparison. Within the mix are some fairly traditional heavy metal riffs and melodies, and the lyrics are so outrageously hostile that they're funny.

But at a Black Flag gig, one wonders if many of the fans even listen to the music or if it is only a convenient backdrop for the crewcutted youngsters to bash each other.

If Black Flag is really the most controversial group in California today, leader Greg Ginn is quite unconcerned about the furor. "There's been all sorts of stuff in the media, really ridiculous stuff," said the softspoken songwriter and guitarist. "Everybody's done his punk rock violence story. You don't see them doing a story about the bar on the corner which might have 100 people and have more fights than we have at a gig with 2000."

Cont'd on page 10

•Black Flag's farewell to Hermosa Beach, June 25, 1981.

April 6, 1981

New Alliance Records
~~116 N. Western Ave Apt. #1~~
San Pedro, ~~CA~~ 90732
~~213-833-8689~~

PO Box 21
San Pedro CA 90733
213 833 8689

Hey Joe,

Very sorry that no more "Cracks in the Sidewalk" EPs are left, it'll be repressed in July (only 1000 were originally pressed).

Coming out in June will be another 12" 45rpm compilation record called "Chunks". Same format as "Cracks...". Will feature Saccharine Trust, Black Flag, Minutemen (All 3 bands each have an album coming out in June on SST records), Artless Entanglements, and new-comers the Slivers (made up of merger between Sharp Corners and Kindled Imagination), Vox Pop, Nig-Heist, the Peer Group, and maybe SWA. (plus the Stains)

Also out in June will be a 7" 45rpm EP by the Slivers called "Restraint for Style".

Okay Joe, write back if you have anything to say, and thanks.

Mike Watt

Thurs
11:00

•New Alliance Records to Systematic Record Distribution, 1981.

7. L.A. Cosmology – You Are Here

In Brendan Mullen's oral history of L.A. punk (more essential reading), Trudie Arguelles, then a young scenemaker up from Palos Verde describes the mid-seventies post-glitter/pre-punk Hollywood scene at Rodney's English Disco:

> "We knew it wasn't the heyday... 'cause we didn't see Iggy or Bowie anywhere. Then we met Rodney and Kim Fowley – any girl that walked in there met them immediately. We also met all these trashy Hollywood kids from broken families, runaways or kids from abused homes... a real sleazy kind of a scene... some of them were really young... and we fit in somehow." (TA, We Got the Neutron Bomb, *Three Rivers*)

And Tito Larriva describes rounding up his bandmate Blank Frank (RIP):

> "I'd pick Blank Frank up for rehearsals with the early Plugz while he was turning tricks on the corner of Highland and Santa Monica Boulevard. That was how he got his junk.... I'd pull up to the corner and say, 'Hey, Frank, you wanna rehearse?'" (TL, *Ibid.*)

In Brendan's other essential oral history, this one of the Germs called Lexicon Devil (*FeralHouse*), Black Randy (RIP), performer and Dangerhouse Records hand, explains,

> "So this excitement started and all these people came out of the woodwork and identified with this new subculture, and everybody had missionary zeal. All of us really wanted something to happen. We also wanted it to happen differently than things always had with these other art movements and subcultures. There was a definite anti-commercial feeling – new forms had to be taken rather than

just new costumes." (BR, Lexicon Devil, *Feral House*)

Black Randy is one of those guys you figure it's just as well you never met. The early Dangerhouse 45s were amazing (Bags, X, Alley Cats, Avengers, Rhino 39, Randoms, Eyes, Deadbeats...); it was the best record label extant! And I bought them for Systematic and started pushing them eastward beginning in 1978. But the singles by Black Randy and the Metrosquad stood out as some kind of anti-art objects akin to Half-Japanese or Swell Maps communiqués, only notably coarse sexually and racially. Their loose jam on the one-sided Yes L.A. compilation was easier to love, but when the first and only Dangerhouse LP was announced as Black Randy and the Metrosquad's "Pass the Dust, I Think I'm Bowie," I asked David Brown, who did the distribution as well as played in the Metrosquad and the Screamers, why Black Randy? He explained that well, he owns the label. And Bowie? Was he important? I gather that was Randy's poke at Darby, and maybe Rodney too.

In Bruce Caen's novelization of the scene, Sub-Hollywood (*Yes Press*) he writes of a certain Black Dick character, "Some people don't care much if they die young and they don't care a damn who they take along with them." In that case, his girlfriend. Rosetta tells me that she first ran away from home at 14 in 1978 – her mother had run off ten years earlier. She got scared at the end of her first night in Hollywood as the clubs closed and the streets emptied. She called home but her sister told her to find her own way back. As fate would have it she wound up staying unmolested at the apartment of Black Randy's guitar player, Bob Deadwyler, who responsibly insisted that she go home and stay out of Hollywood. She did, for another year or so.

Claude Bessy, as a French ex-pat could perhaps see and paint the particular desperation of that Los Angeles best:

> "Some days refuse to end in a decent socially acceptable manner and instead find you driving down factory streets at 4am with hardly no brakes, the steering on it's way, a head full of pills and the Saints or the Misfits or the Germs on your bargain cassette player. Under such conditions, with the dividing line doing multiplications and the glare of other nocturnal comets on wheels snapping chains of blood vessels in your eyeballs you will either end up dead, mangled, arrested or at home. Either way, you've lost. You were meant to find another type of ending, but in the morning you will not remember that you were meant to do anything

> special... and will briefly wonder what drove you as you were driving." (CB, No Mag, #2 1978)

Though some in the South Bay destroyed themselves it was generally a healthier, more purposeful scene. Even the violence coming north from Huntington Beach in Orange County was pretty straightforward compared to the sociopathic viciousness on display in Hollywood where the tone was set by show-biz pedophiles grabbing after young faghags-in-denial chasing reluctant homosexuals back into their closets. I like Jack Grisham's construction – he was the singer in Vicious Circle/TSOL and chief apostle of Huntington Beach punk violence:

> "There were a lot of punkers already hangin' around the South Bay, a bunch of 'em hung around the Black Flag guys, but they weren't fight club dudes at all, they were real nice, real swell guys... they were those peaceful SST types, intellectual punkers who read books and had good political ideas... they were artistic pencil necks to the max. To them it was all about the music and recording... Not like us fuck-ups.... The one measly ethic we were able to scrape up between the four of us in Vicious Circle was that we didn't believe in punk-on-punk violence.... I always respected the old Hollywood punkers. They were real sweet people who went through a lot to make it happen for us fuck-holes in Orange County."
> (JG, We Got the Neutron Bomb, *Three Rivers*)

In L.A., then, you had your choice: physical assault, or mind-fuck. Maybe the worst that can be said of SST at the south bay center of Los Angeles cosmology was that it was the best of both worlds.

Here's Keith Morris describing the earliest days of Black Flag:

> "Greg decided that he wanted to start the band and we needed other players. So, I got a couple of my friends who were just like beach rats that hung out at the Hermosa pier. I'm talking about the guys that came to the party with all of the supplies. One of the guys, the bass player, was from Kansas... Then we had Brian Migdol who was my best friend's little brother. So, what had happened was, the cat from Kansas and Brian spent more time worrying about where they were going to party than they would about rehearsing. And you have to take into consideration that

Black Flag would rehearse six hours a night, seven nights a week. That kind of got a little too much. So these guys were out. And, in the process we found Chuck the Duke... And then we stumbled upon Robo. Robo was living in El Segundo. He was a real freak, totally fit the bill...."
(KM, The Rise and the Fall #9, 2007)

Based on the material in bibliography below, and the memories of Spot and Chuck this might be the best early Panic/Black Flag activity timeline you're likely to see:

Summer 76 – Greg, Raymond, Keith begin jamming. Spot is music writer-photographer for Hermosa Beach's Easy Reader. Chuck's band Würm practices, lives in derelict Bathhouse on the strand.
Aug. 11-12, 76 – Greg and Keith see first L.A. Ramones gig; seeing Joey Ramone sing helps Greg convince Keith to switch from drums to vocals.
Late 76 – Spot and Greg begin jabbering about music regularly in the Garden of Eden.
Early 77 – Panic formed, "Kansas" on bass, Brian Migdol drums.
Mid 77 – Spot jams on bass. Chuck becomes bassist. Regular parties played at Würm-hole on the Hermosa strand. One off-site party played.
Jan. 78 – Media Art recording sessions (Nervous Breakdown).
Early 78 – First club date in L.A., with The Tourists, the McDonald's pre-Red Cross band w/ Greg Hetson on guitar.
Spring 78 – Hawthorne 6th grade graduation party for Steve McDonald w/ The Tourists.
Mid 78 – Migdol quits; Stevenson jams on drums; Robo joins. Bomp! to release Panic EP.
Thru 78 – Aviation Blvd practice pad in North Redondo; parties played there.
Nov. 78 – Name change to Black Flag.
Jan. 27, 79 – Moose Lodge gig on P.C.H. in Redondo, with Alley Cats, Rhino 39; Rodney Bingenheimer attends. First use of Pettibon art on Black Flag flyer.
Feb. 79 – The Last plan to issue Black Flag "Nervous Breakdown" EP, when Bomp! backs out.
Feb. 17, 79 – San Pedro Teen Post with Alley Cats, Plugz, Descendents, Reactionaries.

June 79 – SST 001 released. Black Flag practice at the Church in Hermosa Beach.
June 11, 79 – at Bla Bla Café; 2nd night cancelled.
June 18, 79 – with The Last at Hong Kong Café.
July 12, 79 – possibly the 1st Church party w/ Black Flag, Tourists, and jamming members of Last, Dez, Ron Reyes.
July 22, 79 – with the Tourists at Polliwog Park. Church party that night.
Aug. 12, 79 – at the 2nd Masque.
Sept. 23, 79 – Hermosa cops look into the punks at the Church.
Oct. 1, 79 – Begin recording for album at Media Art.
Oct. 10, 79 – with Dead Kennedys at Mabuhay, SF.
Late Nov., 79 – Keith quits; Ron joins.
Dec. 15, 79 – riot at the Church.

Soon followed the filming of the "Decline of Western Civilization," eviction from Hermosa, SST 002 The Minutemen, etc.
    While the drugging raged in Hollywood and the pummeling continued in O.C., Greg made sure that at SST art ruled... everything: psychology, economics, biology, physics... you name it. Get in the Van includes Henry's tour journals (originally published without photos as Hallucinations of Grandeur, 2.13.61). Henry as the voice of the band seemed to need silence off-stage, so he wrote in his journal. I recall hearing that on one tour it was contagious and they'd all be writing in their journals before and after gigs – Mugger wasn't on *that* tour!
    Read Henry's book and then James Parker's for details on how we contravened Freud, Smith, Darwin, Newton, Ford and one or two other double-domes. (Dave Markey's unreleased documentary on the final Black Flag tour is titled, "Reality 86'd"; bits of it are on youtube.) Check also Tom Troccoli's web-page for insane tourage. Derrick Bostrom's Meat Puppets site offers this on the 1984 Black Flag/Meat Puppets/Nig-Heist tour:

> "We had only two days off, we slept on the floors of strangers and we were making twenty-five bucks a night. We endured arrests, snowstorms and those annoying huge pots of spaghetti the promoters would make to feed us all. (You haven't lived until you try to serve yourself a plate of overcooked pasta while Rollins glowers over you, making sure you don't take more than he feels you deserve.)"
> (DB, meatpuppets.com May 23, 2006)

On the Meat Puppets first tour they had gone out solo. The three of them rolled around the country smoking pot and stopping at art museums in between the gigs. For the Meat Puppets back then the gigs and interviews were collisions with a culture they barely understood. Fanzine and college radio creeps were always looking to separate in their puny minds the other SST bands from Black Flag. They figured they'd never be down with BF but the other bands seemed to be more accessible and carrying less history. We'd gotten back one fanzine where the Meat Puppets had jokingly declaimed any connection to Black Flag or SST, claiming to be on Thermidor instead! Chuck was pissed-off about it and when they called in he asked for the phone, read them the riot act and hung up. I thought, Oh man the umbilical's cut! And I didn't know where they were (No cell phones in the day, kids). But they called right back; they had to! After their second album the Meat Puppets were the only band every other SST band could agree on.

8. The Peopling of SST

Naomi lived with her parents and worked as hostess and bookkeeper at the Black Angus restaurant in Northridge. I often called her there and heard how her voice's professional "warmth" would shift into the genuine personal warmth we all knew. Once Davo drove us up to some Valley gig at Godzilla's and we stopped at the restaurant to pick up some prints; it was a signal moment seeing the sweetest goth girl you ever saw there at her counter in the straight world break into a smile as two of the least likely customers walked in the door. She was an important part of our grand, long-shot, cultural conspiracy and she loved it as we did. Also working at the restaurant was Duff McKagan, and Naomi taxied Guns 'n Roses around town for a period, and later if the straights couldn't be impressed with SST stories she could tell them that Axl had thrown up in her car. She also had Metallica and Nirvana stories to tell – the platinum trifecta!

    Naomi's photo credit was getting known and she had been flown to Chicago to shoot the Effigies, and Naked Raygun, and had visited D.C. and shot bands there already. As a young girl with seemingly little but that to offer, she had thrown herself in front of Black Flag to get inside, but thereafter as SST's working photographer it was she who had the upper hand in her dealings with bands. Bands might now throw themselves in front of her or her camera. In the addendum below, written by Naomi in Europe in 1990, it is she who is recognized by a member of Faith No More. And she writes in her calendar of a May 8, 1992 Soundgarden gig, "Kim really sweet, tellin' everyone who I am & such." Such was Black Flag's standing, and then SST's standing, and finally her own, that rare was the musician who would mistreat Naomi.

    Ray Farrell had come down to SST by 1985 from San Francisco where he'd worked for the Rather Ripped Records store, and Down Home, Rough Trade, Subterranean and other labels and distributors and had done a bizarre KPFA program called "Assassinatin' Rhythm." I had remembered Ray as a true music guy from my years in Berkeley. But it was difficult to convince him to move to L.A. and throw in with SST. He began to promote gigs in Oakland with the Meat Puppets, Minutemen and others. He also managed Panther Burns, and Pell Mell. Farrell came down to the Anti-Club with Pell Mell; Watt had put them on a Minutemen/100 Flowers gig.

The Minutemen were another hot flavor of SST *art brut* and their physically draining, abstract explosiveness was a definite cool-blower for some. Mike Watt writes,

> "As long as D. Boon believed in what we were doing, I didn't give a fuck what anyone else thought. At the same time, it all seemed incredibly funny what we were doing too, like there was some big mistake being made somewhere to allow us to pursue this 'mission.'"
> (MW, Spiels of a Minuteman, *L'oie de Cravan*)

I remember Bruce Licher of Savage Republic (and Independent Project Records) apologizing for a bandmate who, after a shared bill at the Grandia Room, refused to play with the Minutemen ever again. It wasn't being blown off stage so much as having to play to the sophisto-rabble that followed the Minutemen around L.A. These unbeautiful people often ruined fantasies of hipness imported from Europe. In an interview with The Rise and the Fall fanzine Mike Watt talks about how bouncers would regularly try to hustle D. Boon off the stage, sure this character couldn't possibly be in the band! You could call it the L.A. factor, multiplied in the Minutemen's case to the power of San Pedro.

In Hermosa the paranoia ran cool and quiet; in Pedro it flew off the brow like sweat. The paranoia of the waterfront was the first thing John Fante had noticed when he got to Wilmington in the thirties; the Longshoremen's union was the exception in open-shop L.A. and it was under siege and under pressure from the other west coast port chapters to stand up to it.

I always figured that Greg Hurley, brother of the Minutemen's George, must be the King, or rather, General Secretary of Pedro – the raw dude down there minting the lingo, chewing the words up as he spoke them, judging San Pedro's great blue-collar hope, the Minutemen, watching for their slightest move toward the brass ring of superstar-dom (like putting their name on the album cover, or quitting their jobs to tour!). Greg Hurley's art primitivism included early New Alliance label appearances as Kindled Imagination, and the Slivers. This exchange is from an interview he did for D. Boon's fanzine:

> Can you tell me what instruments were used on that Kindled Imagination cut?
> *Flute, perry's pennies, guitar, applezizer, tube, bells, and a variety of other jingley sounds.*
> Voice too?
> *Let's be stupid now.*
> What was Kindled Imagination?
> *Just the kindling of mind... one way to express how exploitation is around everybody in every corner and every area... everybody's getting exploited in one way or another.*
> What do you mean by exploited?
> *Well just like now, you're exploiting me in this interview.*
> (The Prole 1, Nov. 1981)

Hope Greg's doing alright. Hope those around him are too.

Anyway, Pell Mell! This San Pedro/L.A. enervating challenge was getting to the bass player of Pell Mell, who was complaining offstage at the Anti-Club that everyone in L.A. looked ugly and dirty. D. Boon was too sweet-natured to challenge that directly (he explained that his band had a more working class following), but Naomi was there and heard him. "Do I look dirty to you?!," she demanded. Dude got embarrassed and quiet, and then D. introduced Ray to Naomi.

Ray was a stable character, and probably more useful personally to Naomi than I was. In the two years Farrell delayed coming we had rock writer Byron Coley come in weekly to log the radio playlists; but he wouldn't go full-time. We had promised to pay for his gas but that period was one of the worst and we never did and he never complained. Instead he'd bring us a dozen bagels and a quarter pound of cream cheese each trip down. Farrell kept playing hard to get so I would try to get Byron full-time. But he could barely afford to get near us one day a week! Actually it was probably meeting Naomi that convinced Ray to bail on SF; and then Byron took off for Boston and Forced Exposure. Naomi began working at SST full-time in December 1985; actually her office was at Global in Redondo and then Torrance before everything was consolidated in Long Beach in 1987.

We first saw Linda Trudnich, a.k.a., Coughing Disease Woman, at Redondo SST sitting on Pettibon's lap one night after a gig. Her coughing fits didn't seem to phase Raymond. As I recall, the consensus on Linda was rather dubious at first, but Spot reminded me recently that he got volunteered to drive her back to Long Beach that night. He had such a good time talking to her on the drive down that he remembers her even though he was living in Austin by the time she hired on at SST.

Greg's ham-radio mentor had given him Lawndale's P.O.Box 1 back when he launched SST Electronics in the early seventies but the physical office itself was only in Lawndale in the 85-87 period. Linda became the receptionist and copy editor. Linda's sister Heather writes on a British Alice Cooper fansite (sickthingsuk.co.uk) that their parents "were complete hippie, biker types." They knew the Pacific Eye and Ear people who designed many an album cover and their father, Mike Trudnich, met Alice Cooper there and wound up playing the cook on the "Muscle of Love" album cover (it's mislabeled). So Linda had typically loopy Southern California pedigree.

We first knew Kara as Penny. She was Davo-scam, in the parlance, and we'd run across her at some Arizona Black Flag/Meat Puppets dates – May 13, 14, 1983. (See: myspace.com/karanoid for Kara's excellent, illustrated memoir of this.) Davo, like D. Boon with Rapunzel, was stoked to find a girl into punk who hadn't cut her hair. Penny had long hair and a southern accent. She loved the gigs and immediately cut her hair off. A couple years later she found herself running aground in Hollywood and saw that SST bands were at Club Lingerie; she was surprised when Mugger remembered her and even helped her get set up in town. Rob Holzman had just moved out of the house rented by D. Boon, Linda Kite, Jeannine, and their friend Richard (Rob's band Slovenly being the sophistos they were, had moved to San Francisco). On Mugger's recommendation Kara moved in. She got work at a Wherehouse record store in Torrance. I remember stopping by the store with Mugger to talk to her about what she could do to pull SST releases into their bins. Kara writes that she was also taking courses at Harbor Jr. College including one taught by Mr. Ginn:

> "I knew Greg and Pettibon, and literally from the first day in class he would tell these crazy stories about Greg, Pettibon and various friends of his sons during pretty much all of his lectures, and somehow these tales would start out and you would be like what the...? But then they would morph into the point of the lecture. Example, he would say something like, this story, sentence, structure is punk rock and this one is easy listening; this is Jello Biafra, this is John Denver.... He

was such an out there cat. I went home that day and was like, 'D., Greg Ginn's dad is my English teacher!'"
(KN, Aug. 17, 2006)

Regis Ginn was a navigator with the US 8th Army Air Corps during WWII; he met his wife Oie in London – she was an Estonian refugee from the commies. Regis was Catholic, Oie a Christian Scientist. The Mrs. told me that in the military his I.Q. tested at 170; he retired as a Lieut. Colonel. They also served in the L.A. punk rock wars. I can't remember what SST mission Mr. Ginn was helping me out on but as we drove through downtown L.A. on the way back he insisted that I had to see the Bradbury building and I was glad he did – 1890s Los Angeles futurism is nothing to sneeze at. And in December 1981 at Unicorn-SST when I was still new to town and Black Flag was touring east and then to England on the "Damaged" release, I gradually ran out of money and food. I had no wheels, the P.O. Box was in Lawndale, and I didn't have checking account privileges yet, assuming there was any money in the mail. The Ginns didn't forget I was up there working on their son's project. Raymond came up once with some food and suggested there was always Santa Monica Blvd right outside if I got real hungry in the future.

D. Boon was quite the ladies' man. I used to refer to his harem because he was often hanging with a number of girls at the gigs or after. I often would catch a ride up to the gig with him, but could never count on a return ride because the man had duties to perform. He never failed to honk his horn at a pretty girl on the street. Those that turned must surely have been impressed at the blue smoke trailing from his '65 Comet. One day he excitedly told me he'd run into a girl he had known as a kid when they were neighbors. He and Linda Kite set up house almost immediately and we met Linda and her half-sister Jeannine soon after. Spot already knew this Linda because she worked at Recycled Records on P.C.H. in Hermosa and when he drove down to deliver "Jealous Again" EPs he found he'd mistakenly grabbed a box of advance copies of the "Damaged" album which no-one had yet seen. Linda reluctantly chased down his beach bug and turned them over. She said she caught the guys from Slovenly slipping LPs into their L.A. Weeklies – never turn your back on a sophisto, probably stealing New Romantic imports. Linda ran a tight ship but Kara told me D. had her hide candy bars in the bathroom for him.

Jeannine was actually the first girl to work daily at SST. Mugger set her up in 1984 at SST-Hawthorne to do mail-order. She was another good-looking Mexican girl, but quite soft-spoken, even as she fenced with Mugger. And as with Naomi, nobody had to worry about that task again with Jeannine in charge. Harvey Kubernick came down occasionally and it hardly surprised me when Jeannine told me after he'd left that she saw him stuffing cassettes into his pockets. I laughed at the time, but now it strikes me how canny Jeannine was to let him do it!

Kara was right in the middle of the tumult that followed the van crash that killed D. Boon, and paralyzed Jeannine. She'd been invited along on the trip, in fact. She went to the funeral with Mugger and Linda. There were strange rock 'n roll-type threats regarding the funeral and I remember Mugger thinking about asking Henry to help him kind of work the stage for D. I was embarrassed for the Boon family just thinking the funeral might turn into some kind of punk rock event, so I didn't go. Nothing untoward happened. Merrill dropped marijuana seeds into D.'s grave. When Jeannine could she pressed Mugger to replace her with Kara at mail order; Mugger intended to get Jeannine into some computer classes and then re-hire her as soon as possible but she had to leave town so her family could help her. Jeannine has two kids by her boyfriend and lives in Tucson near her mother. Kara did the m.o. and then moved on to do retail sales and distribution. The tag-team of Mugger and Kara could make debt collection fun, shall we say. I'll leave those stories for Kara to tell. (btw, Naomi shot Kara and Jordan for the cover of Black Flag's "Annihilate This Week" EP.)

Raenie recollects that her hiring at SST began with a run-in with Kara:

> "In 1985 I was 17, living with these fucked-up born-again Jehovah's Witnesses in my hometown of San Pedro, and hostessing in a restaurant at Ports of Call in the harbor. I met Kara Nicks at a few parties. We became friends after she accused me of stealing her I.D. and threatened to kick my ass. I think I laughed because I was stoned and I didn't think she really wanted to fight (now I know better!). We didn't fight and she eventually found her I.D. and gave it to me so I could get into the clubs in L.A. and Hollywood to see punk shows. Kara asked me to come to SST in Lawndale one weekend to help Jack Brewer with a bulk-mailing. I remember immediately taking to Jack because he was so sweet and soft-spoken. I would never have guessed this from his performances with Saccharine Trust! Anyway, I worked

> all day Saturday and was called in to interview with Mugger for a regular gig there on Monday. I think the interview went something like this:
>
> Mugger: Hey, foxy, do you want to work at SST?
> Me: Yeah, sure.
> Mugger: Can you drive a big moving van?
> Me: I can drive anything (I was 17 and cocky!)
> Mugger: Why don't you sit on my lap and prove it?
>
> I sat on his lap. Nothing happened. I was hired in 1986 and helped move the offices/warehouse to the Alameda St. location in Long Beach [Jan. 14, 1987]."
> (RK, Jan. 15, 2007)

Raenie worked the mail order and here and there in payroll and merch tables at gigs if bands weren't carrying their own. She quit SST in 1989 when she got pregnant. She said she knew the ten-to-twelve hour days followed by the gigs at night would have to end and knew as well that Los Angeles wasn't the place she wanted to raise her kid. The boy is now 17 himself and drums in a great band called Ogami up in Eugene, Oregon, a kind of polar opposite of San Pedro. Raenie mentioned a recent trip back to Pedro where she was hit with the coarseness of its art scene all over again at a barbeque where even with everyone older and little kids present *la beligerancia continua!*

Another SST girl in this period went by the name Blanche, thereafter as Monica Moran. She chronicled her experiences playing bass in a band (Three Car Pileup) and being pulled into the SST vortex for the fanzine <u>Ben Is Dead</u>. She changed the names "to protect those who didn't know any better," hence, Saffron Trust of leading independent label, STP Records:

> "When Mac Blewer arrived he was alone and in a panic, 'My new record just came in! I need a ride to STP to pick them up. Can you take me?'
>
> I drove him to an old automotive building. I parked my car. Suddenly, Mac then became very serious. He took my hand....
>
> 'There's a guy in there. I want you to keep away from him. His name is BUGGER!'
>
> 'OK, Mac, I will.'
>
> 'Who is this Bugger?' I thought.
>
> My question was quickly answered as Mac and I entered

through the STP Records door.

'Mac Blewer! Hey, everyone, it's Mac Blewer, the ROCK STAR! Hey, Mac, how bout some butt licks? How bout a blow job? Come on, Mac, STICK IT UP MY BUTT!'

That was evidently Bugger.

'Hey, Mac, who's your friend? Some art groupie?'

Mac reluctantly introduced us.

'Can you type?' Bugger asked me.

'Why yes, as a matter of fact I can.'

'Do you want a job?'

'Sure.' I had instantaneously been employed at STP....

I arrived at STP at 9am. I took a seat in front of one of the three computer terminals; the one placed directly below a 'Who's Got the 11 1/4"?' poster. I then asked Bugger what I was supposed to be typing. He then handed me a huge box full of tiny scraps of paper. Each tiny scrap of paper had a name and address on it.

'After you're done with that box, there are fifteen more just like it,' Bugger said.... The inputting of the STP mailing list ultimately took exactly six months. In the course of those six months, every time I entered a name and address, I would try to envision the face of the demented youth who wrote it down....

Various STP recording artists would occasionally saunter through. Every time this occurred Bugger would leap out of his chair and shout, 'HEY LOOK EVERYONE, IT'S THE ROCK STAR! HOW BOUT SOME BUTT LICKS, HOW BOUT A BLOW JOB? COME ON, STICK IT UP MY BUTT!!!'" (MM, Ben Is Dead, Oct./Nov. 1991)

Mugger lives quietly today in a gated community with his wife and son. So I'm guessing Monica is doing okay. She's now a painter in NYC. Pettibon once told me the art world is worse than the record business, so actually, maybe she isn't doing so well at that.

The business end of the label was functioning well for the first time come 1985. Mugger starting taking biz courses at night once he got off the tour crew (May, 1984); if he hadn't done that and taken us legit the IRS or MCI or FBI might have shut us down at any moment. Greg, Chuck, and I would've probably preferred it all stay underground and, strictly speaking, illegal. On that issue Mugger was the grown-up. Sometime after I left, Mugger arranged employee insurance coverage and people even had business cards! (Raenie claims these business cards could get you into some clubs.) Still there was the pressure of the legal bills, and soon losses to distributor bankruptcies – Systematic, Jem, and others. Naomi now made money for each album cover and each promotional shot as well as her wage. By the time SST opened up and signed bands outside its immediate circle like Sonic Youth, Dinosaur Jr., Screaming Trees, etc., getting shot by Naomi on trips to LA was a ritual element of being on the label. Her first session with Dinosaur (pre-Jr.) was at a Safari Sam's date in Huntington Beach (July 1, 1987) with Painted Willie, but when no-one but Naomi showed up, the club told the bands to not play and load back out. Gig became photo session.

Scott Reeder wrote at Stonerrock.com recently that he now regretted not telling Naomi how stoked he was to be shot by her as part of The Obsessed (see the "Lunar Womb" CD). Bucky of the Tar Babies writes that after their first gig in L.A. they were to drive south to stay at Global; Naomi shot the gig and asked them out with a friend afterward. But the responsible boys from Wisconsin worried about getting lost in L.A. and declined; Bucky says that decision haunted him at the time, and then again recently.

I left SST in March, 1986. I stopped by once after leaving and Nan, Watt's ex-girlfriend, was redrafting the SST logo. It had originally been cut unevenly out of construction paper by one of the Church hippies I was told (the S's didn't match). Nan stars in the Minutemen doc, "We Jam Econo"; looks to be doing alright. And while there with Kelley, Linda drove up with Jeannine, so I got to see them too before leaving L.A.

When Black Flag came to an end after the 1986 tour, SST returned to the day-to-day control of Greg and the workload increased to epic, insane proportions. My replacement as production manager, Rich Ford, had to quit playing guitar in Swa as he quickly became the most experienced production manager in the history of the record industry; SST was releasing more titles than any two major labels combined in this period, and this in the era of the three format release – LP, cassette, CD! I hope Rich is okay.

The SST office got wilder in other ways as well. (I'm quite the buzzkill, evidently.) And additional key employees were added. Kara got her boyfriend Craig Ibarra hired into the art dept. in 1987 where he stayed until 1996, later than anyone but Chuck I think; Craig now puts out a great fanzine, <u>The Rise and the Fall</u> (the editorial for issue 2 is titled "We'll be white black after these mexicans!"), and he's working on a book about San Pedro music. Pat Hoed, a.k.a., Adam Bomb from

KXLU was hired about the same time. Others included Chris Takino (RIP) who went on to start the Up label in Seattle. Steve Kall booked for Global then started his own agency. Brian Long worked under Farrell, then was set up in NYC for SST, but instead hired on at Rockpool. I'm guessing Kall's and Long's using of SST made Greg and Chuck harder on the remaining employees. Beth left for Sub-Pop. Debbi? Ingrid? Maria? Others... Victor Gastelum worked in the art dept. after 1992. Robert Vodicka came from KSPC-Pomona and Sounds Good Distribution to run New Alliance from an office in SST, while Ron Coleman ran Cruz records from another office in Long Beach then went to Epitaph.

As the logistical aspects of SST's promotional efforts were enormous, there was at times an entire crew of Mexican illegals who put mailings together beginning in 1985. These shall be nameless, though they are certainly all upstanding amnestied tax-paying citizens by now. SST Records was a regular beacon to the wretched of the earth.

9. Escape from L.A.

When I told my SST partners I was leaving, they asked if I wanted to spend a year in London to put some real attention on the SST label there which booking agent Paul Boswell was piloting part-time. It was an interesting idea and I was glad they asked. It meant the split between Mugger and I, and Greg and Chuck might not have been total. But I was overdue to get back to writing, and London was not where anything was happening in 1986. So I moved back to Chicago in July 86 in time to watch the Machine reconstitute itself under a new Daley and a new, less-Anglophile music scene develop there. I bought a four-flat and worked on it, some screenplays, and Rock and the Pop Narcotic. Four of Naomi's shots are in that book and a number of bands are included due to her input. I counted on her to help me parse all those damn Dischord bands as well as the Wino-damaged metal bands in Maryland (Wino: Scott Weinrich of the Obsessed, Saint Vitus, Spirit Caravan, The Hidden Hand...).

I made a quick five-day trip to L.A. in March, 1988 to help Saint Vitus record "Mournful Cries", which turned out to be their last album for SST. I stopped by SST-Long Beach 1 and had rather awkward chats with Chuck and Greg, but typically friendly reunions with everyone else I'd known, as well as Roseanne's sister Mary who stopped in to see Greg. She was then in a band on New Alliance with Reggie Rector, Phantom Opera.

Raenie had been a classmate of Mary's and said in 8th grade Mary considered herself the school's authority on punk as her big sister was Greg Ginn's girlfriend. (Raenie was judged a poser.) Mugger used to badger Greg and Roseanne to get him happening with Mary when she was still just a rumor. Then suddenly there she was – sweet thirteen – at this gig or that, around SST when Roseanne was around. This was in the run-up to the Black Flag reunion gig at the Santa Monica Civic (June 11, 1983), the last big blow-out in L.A. – three and a half thousand paid for BF/Misfits/Vandals. It was a way for Black Flag to gig big without playing the newest tunes as they were still enjoined from recording. We did old school flyering, or rather everyone but me did. They'd go out at night and get back late: three vehicles, one for each county, to hit high schools, junior highs, and major arteries. They returned covered in wheat paste splatter; Mugger feigned disgust at D. Boon for cumming all down the front of his pants.

We read that the US Festival parking lots would be off limits unless you had a ticket. Apple computers first foray into the music business was in its second year, and was two weekends before our gig and we wanted to get to the car windshields on the Heavy Metal day – *not* the New Wave day. We were sitting around at SST wondering whether to buy tickets for Mugger, Davo, and Merrill and have them smuggle in handbills when I said, "Why don't we fly a plane over it?" Before I even knew whether I was joking, Greg had pulled open the yellow pages to Aerial Banners; I didn't realize that they had flown banners along the beach for Civic gigs before. The US Fest metal headliner Van Halen and the wave headliner The Clash each impuned the other in defense of their rock and roll while Black Flag did the real work of saving the music.

Ron Reyes, a.k.a., Chavo Pederast, was in town to reprise his "Jealous Again" songs, and being a former Black Flag singer he cut in front of Mugger and was instantly squiring Mary around. I gather Mary survived this and being a musician, and I heard she had some kids.

Naomi wasn't around SST the day I visited, and when I got back to Chicago she wrote, asking why I hadn't called her while in town; I winced when I re-read that letter recently. I had talked with Linda about Raymond and my book project and she offered to copy the entire SST press archive for me in her downtime. I got a large box of Xeroxed rockcritiana in the mail soon thereafter. It was invaluable ammo and I sent her a thankyou imitation Pettibon forgery, though I forgot to actually thank her in that book!

I got a call from Kara just as R&TPN was being printed. She had returned to Tennessee for a year and though she was welcomed back at SST in 1990, she found everything changed. The old crew was all gone, replaced by interns and college kids.

 This process ran parallel to the replacements in Black Flag itself for that last tour: Anthony and C'el were fine players but could hardly object if Greg's energy went to his other band, Gone; Henry said, "In 86 there were no soundchecks. We played the same set every night for nine months." (Punk Planet, Sept./Oct. 1997) Greg wasn't done with music, but Black Flag was over. On the penultimate Black Flag album, "Loose Nut," there are Rollins, Kira, Stevenson, and Dukowski-Danky compositions but the last album, "In My Head," is all Greg. I think he considered making it his first solo album instead of the last Black Flag album. Greg tried doing vocals for the first time here but then reconsidered. Unlike on "Damaged" and "My War" the "side two" is here "side one." It's the album he'd been working for since "Damaged," through one barrier after another. A masterpiece. And only Downbeat, and the late blues scholar Robert Palmer seemed to be paying attention. It was some small compensation to be understood by someone who'd written so well about the Muddy Waters band. Henry reprinted Palmer's entire N.Y. Times review in Get in the Van. When I showed that review to Bill, he read it and said, "Who told him all this?"

When Kara was fired by SST at the end of 1990 she was angry and had a specific grievance, but now I see from reading her dispatches that she was most upset at the dismantling of her work-family; SST had taken on the burden of displacing her own uniquely exploded family.

> "I was treated with respect from the SST family and the SST bands same thing; of course you had your assholes but I always felt safe, cared for at an SST show. I think Naomi and Linda felt the same way.... Over the next few years things just kept deteriorating; it was like living my childhood all over again, the harder I tried to hang on the worse it became, and suddenly I no longer recognized my family.... It wasn't until I moved to Nashville in 95 that I quit hating on my experience at SST." (KN, Aug. 16, 2006)

Kara got into speed when it was taking hold of San Pedro and added drinking to it while booking the Springwater and turning it into a music hotspot in Nashville – no small achievement I'd guess. She cleaned up but then was seriously injured in a car accident. She's recuperating from the second reconstruction of her neck and waiting for her lawyer to shake the insurance tree. But Kara's doing okay. Look for her book down the line; you'll be amazed and astounded.

After her accident she began to look for her former SST friends online. She found my piece on Naomi and then found a Social Security death notice for Linda Trudnich. That must have been scary. Kara can't help but lapse into her funny impression of Linda's raw voice and delivery when telling stories of those two bombing around L.A. on

Kara's motorcycle. She also does a good impression of Linda's old country Nana, yelling warnings after Leenda! Hearing about Linda from Kara I asked around and Ray Farrell wrote,

> "I saw Linda about 3-4 years ago at an SF Sacc Trust/SY gig. She was not in good shape.... I asked her if she was using drugs and she replied that if they weren't so expensive she would be." (RF, Aug. 8, 2006)

Mugger wrote remembering having to fire Linda over her drinking at SST. She then worked at XXX Records in Hollywood before moving north to the bay area with a boyfriend. Kara tracked down Linda's sister Heather and found out that Linda had died of lung cancer in a hospice (see her memorial card nearby).

It was interesting to hear about Naomi from those who worked at SST after I left. "Naomi Petersen" was of course well established as a photo credit by the end of 1983 to those buying and wearing out copies of the early SST releases, and reading fanzines. And by 1985 she was a recognized L.A. fixture. Kara felt intimidated by Naomi at first, and assured me that this was rare for her. Mugger told Kara that she had more in common with Naomi than she knew. Raenie thought Naomi had it all together and felt slightly embarrassed to be drinking a beer while working the merch table at a gig when Naomi seemed to be on the job doing without – both after putting in long days at SST. Kara writes,

> "Raenie says the reason I was so sketchy when Naomi first came over to LB SST was because she was Global (read: one of them!). Paranoia ran rampant at SST." (KN, Aug. 16, 2006)

Ibarra writes,

> "I always thought Naomi was one of the coolest people working there. I used to go into the office she shared with Jordan Schwartz and trip out on all the photos she had plastered on her wall next to her desk." (CI, Sept. 21, 2006)

When I saw Jordan in 2005 we didn't actually talk too much about Naomi; he seemed a bit shell-shocked over the recent death of Kim Pilkington and when he and Dave Markey told me the details I could understand (see their book, Party with Me Punker, *Abrams*). Kim appears in some of the Markey films and she went out with Mugger for a while. Jordan assured me that working for Greg and Chuck had prepared him for the corporate world!

Debbi writes that she considered Naomi a larger than life figure and Kara added "Naomi was more rock star than the rock stars." That places her with Mugger and Spot, who I told <u>Ego Trip</u> magazine, were easily mistaken for the rock stars when they and Black Flag rolled up in Anytown, U.S.A. on those early tours. Kara also writes,

> "One of the first things that drew me to the whole underground scene was that it appeared to be more liberal and open-minded. How wrong I would turn out to be. Naomi, Linda and I (as well as other real women) would discuss this years later, how we were often treated in this business, we were more often than not treated like groupies, or hangers-on. This really hurt us. Don't get me wrong, it's not like any of us were running around trying to set some example.... Other chicks are brutal and when Naomi and I finally started talking to one another (instead of the polite nod w/ a bit of conversation) we discovered we really had more in common than not." (KN, Aug. 16, 2006)

Safe in Chicago, I would talk to Naomi by phone and we wrote each other. She writes twice in late 87-88 that she was trying to cut her SST hours down to 50 a week! Brave girl. Naomi was preparing a move to Washington, D.C. for years it seemed. One letter is written at the end of an 11-hour shift at SST, another at 3:53am before turning in. In another she complains of putting in 126 hours on her last two-week SST paystub, though her solution is to add a part-time restaurant job to break up the monotony! These restaurant jobs were important to her; I've seen snapshots of her at their Halloween parties, or her going-away parties complete with "We'll Miss You Naomi" banners on the walls. The crews all look like such nice normal people! And it seems clear that Naomi was always the star of the staff.

She was no longer having much fun at SST and wasn't going out to shows much. She wrote that working with Ray Farrell was the only thing keeping her there. And then he was gone (Feb. 8, 1988). So Naomi left. Mugger and Jordan too. Then the rest. Ultimately even Chuck – gone! (A wild guess: No farewell parties...) Naomi had friends at Dischord Records and she was looking forward to getting out of Los Angeles. To the extent I still worried about Naomi, I worried less thinking she would be in Jeff Nelson and Ian MacKaye's orbit. She wrote that Chuck and Mugger were paranoid about her going to work

•Before Naomi appeared, I tried to shoot bands; Black Flag practice at Target Video, SF, Jan. 1983. Naomi processed this roll. (JC)
•Naomi at Minor Threat, July 11, 1982, Dancing Waters, San Pedro. (Kevin Salk)

•Naomi's December.

•Toshio's 1980 gift. (CP)
•Minor Threat w/ Robo, Henry, Unicorn-Santa Monica, July 1, 1982. (NP)
•With friend Vickie, Stuart Anderson's, Northridge, circa 1982.

•Monitor, circa 1978: Jeff, Anne, Michael, Steve, Laurie; gallery performance, No Mag #2.
•Saccharine Trust, March 6, 1982, Unicorn practice space party, Santa Monica, l-to-r, Greg, Chuck, Ken Starkey, Bill, Joe, Henry, Lisa Roeland, Vic Mary Cooper, Nan Roeland, Jim Garner, Martin Tamburovich. (Jordan Schwartz / wegotpowerfilms.com)

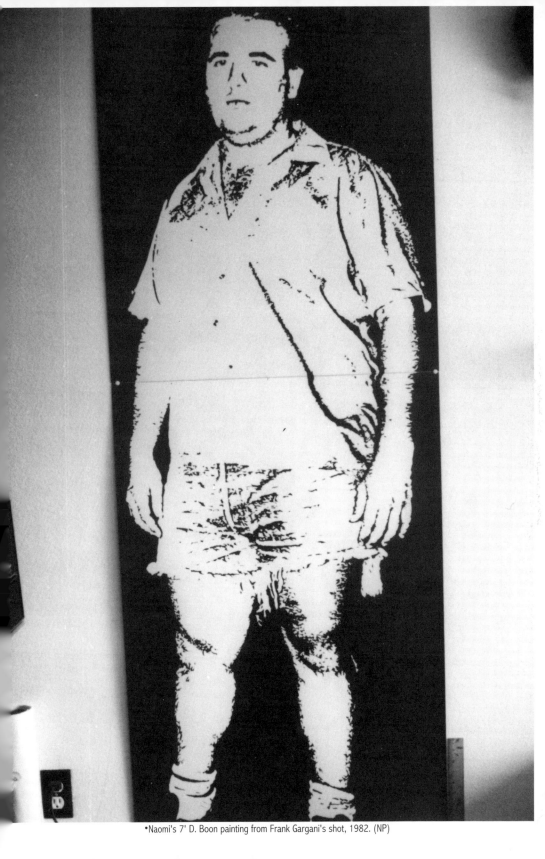
•Naomi's 7' D. Boon painting from Frank Gargani's shot, 1982. (NP)

•Aug.1981 flyer; Henry's 2nd show out, Raymond Pettibon art.

•Oct. 1981 flyer, Frank Navetta art.

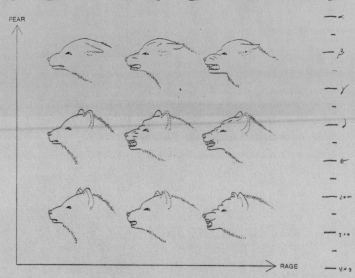

•Dec, 1981 flyer, Laurie O'Connell art.

The Return of the Amazing, $
"New Improved; Killer; ⊗

STAINS

Friday Night... After Hours
Doors open 12:00
Punk Metal DREAM FROM E LA
Media Blitz 5

STAINS PARTY
At: The Final CLUB

Just back from countless (!) sold out shows in San Francisco!
No SHIT!!

1600 ARGYLE
Hollywood; EL LAY —
(CATHAY DE GRANDE)
B.Y.O.B.
JUNE 10, 1983
D.J. Stella

FRIDAY Night - June 10th '83
After Hours - The Band will go on at 2 AM
Fuck U!

•June 1983 flyer by Ceasar Viscarra, or Jesse Fix.

•Spot & D. Boon, 1984.
•Ian at Dischord house with Tomas Squip, 1984.
•Grant tries to reason with paparazza at KXLU with Stella, 1985.
(All NP)

- The Meat Puppets, Total Access Studio, Redondo Beach, April 1983.
- The Dicks, Cathay de Grande, Hollywood, 1984.
- Hüsker Dü, Rhino Records, Westwood, 1985.

(All NP)

Oregon Picture Print

FIRST LARRY LEFT TOWN, THEN THE JUG BAND BROKE UP, THEN THE DRUGS RAN OUT AND I MOVED IN W/ JILL WILSON WHO RAISES RABBITS IN TIGARD, WORKS DOWNTOWN AS AN ACE TYPESETTER. WE LIVE IN THE BASEMENT — THE HOUSE ABOVE ORIGINALLY A HOUSEBOAT ON THE RIVER NEAR CANBY. MOVED HERE WHEN THEIR COMMUNIST COMMUNE DISSOLVED IN '49; ALL OF WHOM MIGRATED WEST FROM BLACK MOUNTAIN COLLEGE IN N. CAROLINA, LEGENDARY CENTER 4 BEATNIK LITERATURE, RAWHOUSE, MODERN DANCE, PAINTING, ETC. HOUSE OWNERS NOW IN SUDAN 4 STATE DEPT. I'M WORKING AS A PHONE SALESMAN. MORE SOON

503 244 8723
10604 SW 55TH AVENUE
PORTLAND 97219

To:
JOE CARDUCCI
SST ELECTRONICS
PO BOX ONE
LAWNDALE, CALIFORNIA
90260

SKYLINE and INNER HARBOR — Baltimore, Maryland

Hey Joe,
The tour going good. The gig in Trenton was really dumb. Our opening band was heavy metal named Krank. They even spit fire at the end of the set. Our morale is good, although Mike was blown up a few times. We'll be OK. How's the label doing. Everyone asks about our new album. Get it happening dude! See ya in Sep. Tell Kelly I said hello.
D. Boon

Joe Carducci
c/o SST Records
P.O. Box 1
Lawndale, CA 90260

Scene looking north down Sitton's Gulch from Cloudland Canyon towards New England, Ga. at Cloudland Canyon State Park, 8 miles south-east of Trenton, Ga., off U.S. Hwy. 143.

Joe & Mugger,
Atlanta was fuckin' overwhelming. After being in the big swamp of the earth (FLA.) for so long, seeing the minutemen was exhilarating. We met them in Jacksonville Beach then we went to miami (hotels galore) stayed here one nite then up to Atlanta for the weekend. That was their best show in the South. The tour pace is not my idea of living. We'll meet again in New Orleans — then while they do TX. I'll be in Boulder (my Dad's) and we'll meet in Albæ and see ya then. Love, Linda & Jeannine

Post Card
SST Records
P.O. Box 1
Lawndale, CA.
90260

•News from Dave Lightbourne in Portland, 1982.
•Word from D. Boon on tour, 1984.
•Word from Linda Kite & Jeannine in Fla., 1984.

Joseph, my little love bug.   1.28.85

I was talkin' to yr little angel, "Tigger" Corben, the other night and he was tellin' me how you'd become a big-time record producer w/all the accoutrements: big smokin' stogies, blood-stained tiger-skin couches, hemmaroids the (exact) size of Greg's fist, etc. Sounds like quite a life yr leadin' there, stud.
And o' course, since yr so busy tryin' t' get milk pourin' from the spouts o' those Lawndale cuties, you've no doubt forgotten yr old playmate, Byron.
So here I sit in my lonely apartment, dreamin' o' the days before I lost my copies o' Vitus, Meat Pups 1, Punchline and Butt Fires. Oh, those were the days my friend, we thought they'd never end, we'd sing and laugh for ever and a day, la-la-la-la-la-la, la-la-la-la-la-la...
Man, it's enough to make me "hear" birds chirpin' in the way fuggin' cold air outside the sun room (so called) in which I'm typin' this thing. Anyway, life on the East Coast's pretty much as bland as sand and if I don't get a job soon (I've tendered applications w/both Arco Gas and Heartland Market, so hope springs) then this book deal I've had brewin' better come through. What that's supposed t' be's a semi-quickie on Canuck visionary/splatter director David Cronenberg. These women editors in NYC contacted me 'bout doin' it 'round six weeks ago and I sent 'em a ten pg. summary w/chaptyer breakdowns, but they haven't found a publisher yet. Shit. Freelancin's been slow, but I've been tryin' t'get it more in gear since the new yr. Speakin' o' which, please lemme know when either BF or the Minuteboys'll next be in B'ton. Supposedly they'll let me do a live review of either of 'em for this teen rag called STAR HITS. The only reason they wouldn't let me do this last MM thing was 'cause they didn't have one o' their own photogs there. Who can figure it.
Been doin' lotsa work w/Jimmy Johnson on revivin' FORCED EXPOSURE. We've so far got stuff on Sonic Youth, Big Black, Velvet Underground, Samhain and the Gun Club w/poetry by Howard Wuelfing and some short stories by Michael Gira from the Swans. Hopin' t' get some writin' outta Hank and a drawin' outta Raymond, along w/much other crap, but we'll see. If you've got any short written stuff you'd care t' submit, I'd like t'see it. And if ya don't have any right now, just lemme know if y'ever do since we're hopin' t' regularly run non-music stuff in FE and I'm startin' t'collect the first ish o' BOHUNK too.
Anyway, I gotta scram and pick the little woman up from work, but if I could get the above disks AND ALSO THIS H. DU 45 I'VE BEEN HEARIN' 'BOUT I'd be a happy gent. If not, I'll just sigh some more.
So, I'll be seein' ya in May or June most likely.
'Til then, I remain
Yr Pal

Byron

XX OO
to "Tigger" too

•Byron Coley lost to the east coast, 1985.

at Dischord with all she knew. She did expect to work at Dischord but her fulltime gig was lined up with the reggae label, Ras Records. Ras was to release a record by her friends, Scream, then managed by Glen Friedman who was now in New York shooting hiphop.

Here are her last west coast and earliest east coast calendar entries [parentheticals by me]:

> "**Apr. 9, '89**: *Partei bei* McGee's [LB restaurant going away party for Naomi – see photo]
> **Apr. 10**: Moving day. [4 day drive w/ her father]
> **Apr. 15**: Holy Rollers @ DC Space. Lose truck!
> **Apr. 16**: Ian's B-day
> **Apr. 17**: go to RAS-meet w/ Gary-start next Monday! Go to Dischord
> **Apr. 18**: fIREHOSE & Senator Flux@930 Club. <u>GREAT</u> show! Car accident!
> **Apr. 19**: call Knappers! Seth calls. Talk w/ Chuck. Start @ Dischord. Phone hooked up! David 1st call! Call Chris B. good chat. Mark called! Wasn't home!
> **Apr. 21**: talk w/ Stabb- asks me to be G.I. mg.!! Call Vick. Ich bin erkäklet!
> **Apr. 22**: call David. Screaming Trees @Maxwell's <u>GREAT</u> show!! Talk w/ Damens, Sonics & mehr! Good talk w/ Mark. <u>Long</u> drive home!!!
> **Apr. 23**: Screaming Trees@Georgetown Univ. S.Trees ok but others schlecht! Trees back to NYC-good chat w/ Mark. Call Pen-<u>good chat</u>! So <u>müde</u>! Call David-hasn't received either letter! Talk w/ Stabb! Rain
> **Apr. 24**: Start@RAS! 9:30 Seth calls-job at Dischord looks no go – oh well." (NP, 1989)

She hit the ground running... She had been going to less gigs in L.A., now she was everywhere in her new stomping grounds.

Naomi's letters also reveal her insight on the music of this or that band at a particular stage in their evolution. (How many folks on earth besides her understood just how incredible Baiza's second band, Universal Congress of, had suddenly gotten? Or how the Tar Babies records didn't quite prepare you for what they put out live?) I found such musical sophistication, as opposed to mere stylistic handicapping, to be common only around SST.

It shouldn't surprise that the girls at and around SST were far hipper than the music professionals of that day; it's our loss that they are not asked or will not answer and so are un-represented in the articles, books and films coming out. The Minutemen documentary, "We Jam Econo," really only features Nan and Kira in amongst all us aging rock guys, when I can think of at least ten more girls that should be in there for all the Minutemen gigs they saw, all the bowls they smoked with them, not to mention all the miscellaneous whathaveyou.

Raenie characteristically describes her record store experience in musical terms:

> "I worked at a record store for a real long time and was pleasantly surprised when one day I realized that people listen to music differently. That realization made me the antithesis of the record store snob, but really opened my mind in terms of appreciating other people's tastes in music, while finding common threads throughout genres."
> (RK, Jan. 19, 2007)

I know from my experience at Systematic trying to sell the better stuff to shop-buyers how rare such intelligence is among nominal music fans. It's easier to feel smart if you just close down your world. The girls we knew chumped the record geeks and movement punks and rockcrit wannabes.

One night after Saccharine Trust at the Anti-Club, I found myself standing with three of the hippest – Kelley, Teresa, and Rosetta – as I put away my tape recorder. Naomi stepped over as she capped her lens and Kelley said, "Look, Carducci, all your followers are here!" I don't think I blushed, but I pressed my followers on whether they would kill for me, and they all eagerly offered that they would, gladly. (Daphna, you do not know how lucky you were.)

Kelley is now a talent agent; she and her speed-dial cabal had a hole blown through it when Rick Van Santen died a few years ago. I last talked to Rick on the phone during the Bulls/Lakers finals in 1991. Rick affected something like a wimp manner but he loved sports. Pettibon and I often met him and Kelley at the Forum for Kings or Lakers games, or at Dodger Stadium where Kelley could occasionally get KIIS FM's dugout box seats. Rick often flew to the away games for the Lakers playoffs with Greg. (Rick said Greg had been reading my book on the plane.) The Lakers had won game one but I fearlessly assured Rick that the Bulls made adjustments better than any other team and could very well win the next four straight, which they did; Rick must've thought I was insane, then a genius. Kelley said recently that she'd never get over Rick's death, but she was angry as well at him for behavior she considered refusing to grow up. I first saw her when I was new to SST in the West Hollywood office above Unicorn. She came in with a mixed drink in her hand at eleven in the morning to talk to Greg. I'm sure Kelley still thinks to call Rick ten times a day, but she herself, amazingly enough, is doing great.

I caught Rosetta last year just before she left L.A. for Kentucky with her husband. As she filled me in on her recent history, I flashed on the X song, "Los Angeles," and she nodded knowing full well... She looks good, is happily married, but was bitter that the black and brown street vibe had forced her to quit working due to the harassment she received on the bus home every night. She told me one hellacious punk rock story after another and I of course demanded she write a book. She rejected that idea saying, "I'm not an asshole; I'm a racist." Claude Bessy also said that L.A. was turning him into a racist. Mr. Ginn thought it a funny left wing idea that everyone was a racist, and so whenever Marcus Allen or Eric Dickerson broke loose for a big run he'd say, "Look at that racist run!"

Now in her bluegrass wonderland Rosetta tends animals and a garden and follows the horses – schooled by Raymond no doubt. She just wrote that there's been talk about her at the general store, "Who was that woman at the livestock auction? Is she a single gal and what is her nature?" Rosetta is still in touch with Exene and some others. She told me she couldn't imagine that Teresa might still be alive. When Henry split from their Lawndale house in summer 1982, Rosetta invited Teresa to move in and she got a good look at the careless way she moved through the world. Teresa was often staying at some sleazeball straight guy's place. One night we were starving at SST when she called from Long Beach. She conned Davo (or was it Mugger?), Spot and I down there with promises of food; there was nothing but a box of Cheerios in that whole stylin' pad, which we ate dry. She didn't want a ride back up to Redondo; she was just lonely. Teresa can be seen in Friedman's shot of Black Flag playing the Suicidal Tendencies party, Apr. 30, 1983, in Get In the Van (pg. 93, 2nd ed.). It's also in Glen's book, Fuck You Heroes (*Burning Flags*); she's sitting on the left with Kelley laying her head on her knee, while they watch Black Flag burn. Davo is on the right edge of the shot – it was Dez's last gig with Black Flag. Dez went to Redd Kross, replacing Tracy who always seemed to be nodding off as she wailed, definitely the coolest hottest druggy of that day – married now, raising a kid. Dez soon put together D.C.3. with Kurt from Overkill on drums and Kira on bass; Kurt's on the first album but Kira was heisted by Greg and her brother Paul added on keyboards; even without a bass their debut is a very powerful album. A couple guys from the Stains, Ceasar and Louie filled out the band thereafter.

Rosetta also said she thought Gerber was running out her string finally. Kelley used to fret about Gerber ignoring her doctor who'd told her she was one stiff drink from liver failure and death, and Gerber was then just 25! And yet, there she is in Brendan's book – one of the wilder voices in it.

Michelle Bell, called Gerber "because of my forehead," had an Austrian mother who married her soldier father and moved to Georgia, then San Diego. Father left and then she moved with her mother to Los Angeles in 1973 at the age of thirteen. Here's Gerber from 1983:

> "No Mag: Have you rehabilitated?
> Michelle: Not completely. I still think, well, there's the bar, I think I'll go get a Stolichnaya, and then get really drunk and see what kind of trouble I can get into.... I was real rebellious against my parents. When I moved out I was like a devil or something. I was like this wild offspring that got thrown out into the world. I went crazy at first. I felt there were no limits whatsoever. Of course the whole scene that I was into was just that... no limit magnified!" (MB, No Mag, 1983)

There are classic photos of Gerber in Lexicon Devil, but I remember her hanging around SST-Redondo in 1982 when she was with Chuck Biscuits; seemed she could tone it down to his daytime level of beer-sippin' and sunflower seed chewing.

There are some great Kira Roessler interviews around lately in Citizine, and Razorcake fanzines. Razorcake also tracked down Alice Velasquez (the Bags) for an amazing debriefing on how an immigrant's daughter who spoke no English until grade school skipped assimilation and went directly to the Hollywood punk scene (see also the Alice Bag Band in "The Decline"). At Alicebag.com there's some great material including original interviews with notable L.A. women. Here's something from the interview with Nicole Panter, (then wife of artist Gary) manager of The Germs, and actually the most striking presence in "The Decline" film:

> "During the Elks Lodge Riot, Lorna (Doom) and I were coming out of the rest room – in true contrarian punk fashion, we'd gone into the men's room – just in time to see the cops working their way up that huge wide grand

staircase in a wedge. They were holding up thick Lucite shields with one hand and just whacking the hell out of people with their billy clubs as they moved up the stairs.... The Go-Go's were onstage, I think. We worked our way through the audience telling people to leave through the stage exits, to get out of there because the cops were going crazy. We went... out the stage doors only to walk into what looked like downtown Beruit. There were sharpshooters on every rooftop spaced three feet apart from each other, hundreds of them, and the ever-present helicopters with their spotlights, and up and down on the sidewalk, the swat squad was in full riot gear, like the guys who'd come up the stairs and they were just wailing on people. It was something I never hope to see again in my life."
(NP, Alicebag.com, Apr. 2005)

In a 2002 memoir titled, Coloring Outside the Lines (*Rowdy's*), Aimee Cooper adds to the thin shelf of female testimony. She worked at Slash and was a resident of TC house in Hollywood, which was a crashpad for young Germs insiders set adrift by Darby Crash's suicide. They were evicted and got another house on Oxford Ave. which was a way-station for Black Flag between the Torrance SST and the Unicorn SST in West Hollywood. It's also where Black Flag found their drummer for 1982, Emil McKown. Aimee opens her book by describing her disappointment at seeing the Rolling Stones from a distance at an outdoor concert in California (likely the same Anaheim show that Chris took Naomi to), and then later her thrill on seeing the Heartbreakers in a virtually empty club in the Village.

The oral histories Please Kill Me, and We Got the Neutron Bomb feature dozens of amazing female voices. And Brendan tells me that Naomi was on his list but he couldn't find her. Jenny Lens also writes that she was deputized to find Naomi for the "We Jam Econo" filmmakers and couldn't. She was alive then but other than her posting some bios of her friends' bands on the All Music site, she seems to have not been involved with music at all.

In researching this book, I got to see some of the girls from back then. Hearing what they made of what went on was quite a privilege. I'm not much of a reporter but then I wasn't going to point a microphone at old friends. I did encourage them all to do interviews when people asked and write their own stories. I don't think they will.

10. Acknowledgements II

At gigs around L.A. – the big ones (Santa Monica Civic, Olympic Auditorium), the halls (Perkin's Palace, Country Club, Palladium, Longshoreman's, Ukrainian, Alpine Village, Godzilla's, Dancing Waters, Fender's), the bars (Al's, Whisky, Cathay, Anti-Club, Music Machine, Wong's West, Raji's), the one-offs (Eddie's Café, Grandia Room, El Señorial, Mi Casita), the outdoors scams (Manhattan strand, the Federal Building, San Pedro Fish Fiesta, Wilson Park, Angel's Gate Park, UCLA), the house parties (God knows where) – I saw the guys who were playing and the guys who came out to see their brother-bands; it was a warped anti-social scene where partyers mixed with sociophobes, artists mixed with delinquents, druggies mixed with teetotalers. And that was just SST.

I'd also run into some of the quiet characters that had come to this loud music for perhaps similar reasons. We'd pick up where we last left off, talking about their bands or who they'd seen recently and what new records were out. It was always great to run into Janet Hausden (Disposals, Redd Kross), Janice Jones (Disposals, Nip Drivers), Joey 8head Halzman – RIP (Invisible Chains, Neon Veins), Ceasar Viscarra (Stains, D.C.3), Crane, Dirk and John (Tragicomedy), Kjehl, John and Kevin (Urinals / 100 Flowers), Keith Mitchell (Monitor, Romans, Opal, Mazzy Star), Michael Uhlenkott (Monitor, Romans), Juan Gomez (Human Hands, Romans), David Wiley – RIP (Human Hands), Fredrik Nilsen (BPeople), Mark Wheaton (Chinas Comidas, Johanna Went), Kurt Schellenbach (Nip Drivers), Bruce Licher, Stuart Sweezey, Colleen Pancake, Dave Travis, Dave Van Heusen.... Others of somewhat higher voltage included Rosanne and Mary Bojorquez, Greg Hurley, Debbie Patino, Mike Webber (RIP), Reggie Rector, Louie Dufau (RIP), Ed Danky (RIP), Mike Quercio, Al the Pal, Greg the Pope, Mike Brinson, Jason Golliher, Marlon Whitfield, Steve Stiph, Modi Frank, Jennifer Schwartz, Sue Noorthoek, Mike Muir – these I might easily bore but they respected me as an extension of Black Flag, Mugger, Pettibon,

Spot, Minutemen, Saccharine, *et. al.*

    I would also run into our version of music industry professionals like Rick Van Santen (RIP), Craig Lee (RIP), Al Flipside, Geza X, Glen Friedman, Ed Colver, Bruce Kalberg, Harvey Kubernik, Robbie Fields of Posh-Boy, Gary Stewart and Nels Cline of Rhino, the Hein brothers and Robbin Naggatoshi of Greenworld-Enigma, Bob Say of Jem/Moby Disc, Bo of Bomp!, Stella, and Carmel. Occasionally Keith Morris would stop by SST-Phelan, when the coast was clear, to pick up a record and check out the scene.

    Van Santen, according to Brendan Mullen's obit in the L.A. Weekly, got his start as a kid manning the Screamer's merch table. (There was Screamers merchandise?!) Rick started booking the Whisky and the Roxy when he could not even legally attend the gigs. He was a good friend of Pat Smear, Kelley, Kira and Paul Roessler and loved Black Flag. He helped us break the LAPD's ban on Black Flag; Rick put them on unannounced in both clubs with Twisted Roots. The Whisky set (July 20, 1982) seemed powerful to me and I was surprised how disappointed Greg was afterwards, but I listened back to my tape and then I could hear what bothered him. But in the audience the set had seemed a bristling return to Hollywood – yes, certainly, but that part was theater, not the music played. You learned a lot around Greg if you could stand the pitilessness of his intellect. At times after sets the rest of the band needed you to say the gig was hot just to build back up what Greg had just torn down. It was no lie because the gigs, the checks, the practices were always hot. But that's not it.

    What struck me at the Roxy (Aug. 7, 1982) was the soundcheck. The place was empty but for some of the bands and our crew. Performance artist Johanna Went who then had an excellent rockin' improv band (check the Posh-boy LP) was sitting on the floor in front of the stage stuffing her giant props while Black Flag set up their equipment. At Spot's command ("Ahhh, what the hell...") they began to check with their newest song, though "Slip It In" as yet had no lyrics. I came to love the tune as an instrumental due to these soundcheck performances. So Henry was on stage merely responding to the playing. Johanna stopped what she was doing and stared. You could almost see her thought: *That's Black Flag?!* That song sounded so massive with the Biscuits/Dez five-piece line-up that I started taping.

    Between songs on my cassette I hear Joe Baiza telling me about his new apartment and not noticing D. Boon calling him; Baiza was on the Minutemen's guest list as their roadie so I remind D. to address him as

"Roadie," which D does and then Baiza does a Stepin Fetchit, "Oh, oh sorry boss!" After BF plays "Jealous Again," you hear Merrill laugh, "Are you taking off your pants, Baiza, what you doin'?!" Joe responds, "I'm just getting comfortable." D. and I laugh. At the end of Black Flag's check ("I Can't Decide"), into the sudden silence D. looks up from tuning his guitar and offers up the weak stoner cheer, "New Wa-a-a-ve!" Mugger is still calling Greg "Lurch" and all is right with the world.

Driving another nail in the coffin of the LAPD blacklist was Gary Tovar. We met him in Goleta, near Santa Barbara, when he put on a Black Flag/Adolescents/Channel 3/Overkill gig. We managed to make the news in that broadsheet up there courtesy a Pettibon flyer that happened to reference a particularly sick rape-mutilation that had shocked the Santa Barbarans – naturally we drove up there twice and glued it, and then a follow-up flyer Raymond did commenting on the coverage, all over their fake adobe downtown. (See the flyers on pgs. 50-51 of Get in the Van, 2nd Ed.) The gig went off great; it was the first time I got to see Overkill and they were so damn good – the best punk-fueled commercial hard rock/metal band there ever was, only they didn't last long enough for the commerce to commence.

Greg and Chuck figured if Gary could handle the pressure to cancel that gig, he might be the guy to set up in L.A. for concert promotion. We talked it over and he was all for it, but he seemed to want to seal the deal with a camping trip up in his neck of the woods. His little sister hoped to get her hands on Henry but there was no chance he was going anywhere near Gary's peace pipe pow-wow. I remember Greg begging Mugger and I to go along while Chuck just grinned. Greg thought me and Mugger would somehow be able to keep he and Chuck from smoking pot. Like I wanted that job! They went; Greg got high and never came down. Thanks Gary!

Musicians believe that pot speeds their sense and so effectively slows down music, giving them more time to approach the beat and place their playing where in the rhythm they want it. I don't believe this but they all do, so Greg surely felt his playing improve or he wouldn't have kept smoking the stuff. I think pot's effect plays out in the paranoid realm of the performer more generally. And then the guitar itself is the all-time great procrastination energy sink. Guys all across the country are getting real good on their guitars as they shine all the shit their moms or girlfriends expect them to be doing around the house.

Getting up on stage is a confrontation with paranoia – making it real, facing it, and perhaps earning it. Pot probably makes the anticipation of that moment when one must step out on stage easier but it exacerbates everything else. In Black Flag's case, Greg probably grew more dissatisfied with Chuck, Henry, Bill, and Kira, not to mention his family and us flunkies. I don't think it occurred to Greg that the feeling might be mutual all around because we just didn't have that kind of standing with him.

Anyway, Goldenvoice was the company which Gary, and later Rick, turned into a dominant promoter. Right away Gary began to ignore us when we asked to get a band on his bills. But they were mostly hardcore slamaramas at the Olympic Auditorium in the early days so it was no big loss. And he came around once they got access to better venues. Dave Rat says Gary preferred Rat Sound because their PA columns weren't easy for the stage-divers to climb. Their third partner, Paul Tollett, assured me it was a trip building up that company to a dominant all-purpose rock promoter with characters like Rick and Gary. The cheesy Chinese restaurant style font that Chuck used on one of the flyers remains the ubiquitous Goldenvoice logo. The feds managed to put Gary in jail for a time; hope he's doing okay.

Jack Marquette at the Anti-Club, and Brendan Mullen at the Club Lingerie also helped our bands play to new people. And record stores in those years were probably the most important medium. Zed in Long Beach and Poobah's in Pasadena were important outlets, as were Vinyl Fetish, Bomp!, 2nd Time Around, Moby Disc, Middle Earth, Be Bop, and of course, Tower – if only they'd been a national chain back then! Tower's recent extinction may prove a deathknell for more than just the hippest Cali merchant dream, begun by Russ Solomon in a corner of his dad's Sacramento drugstore in 1960. Seven years ago the major labels cut Tower a year's slack to keep them in business, now the record business can't even save itself. American music was once so strong a cultural process that the abuse it suffered at the hands of the creepazoids who ran the labels and the radio stations didn't seem to show. And now? Did the parasites finally kill the host, or was the music weakening anyway? Farrell quotes Greg as saying, "There are no saints in this business." That sounds right, but there's sure plenty of martyrs...

If I remember right, Kubernik wired up Deirdre O'Donoghue (RIP) to an early Rollins spoken word performance and she promptly went nuts over the whole lot of us – well, most of us. She found a way to present a lot of what we did to KCRW listeners in its formative period. She was a pro who'd started at WBCN at Boston in 1974. Alas SST couldn't save public radio music programming from its eclectic yuppie doom – as a music purveyor today they're just slightly edgier than Starbucks. But Deirdre helped us buff the label's profile and get bands into styler joints like McCabe's, and UCLA.

Henry's "Family Man" piece was recorded at her program. He also did it as a video with Randy Johnson. They made two others I think; Randy also made three Minutemen videos and a Black Flag one and parlayed that into writing "The Doors" script for Oliver Stone and a thousand page script for the videogame "Gun." The Pettibon on the cover of "Family Man," captioned "November 23, 1963," features a suburban dad killing off his family the day after. Raymond used likenesses of his nephew Alex (a.k.a. Nelsin) and niece Janet (a.k.a. Merica). Alex had a band called 1208 on Epitaph with Pettibon art on the cover. Janet when she was little would get nervous when the van pulled up outside the house. Mr. Ginn would set her off by announcing, "Here come the punks!" and then calm her by saying, "Nonsense, Merica, Black Flag are the good guys." That's how Harvey ends his liner notes on the album, "Black Flag are the good guys. How many of them are left?"

These folks I knew and many more I did not, made Los Angeles the place to be. And now I look over the faces in the audiences in the old live shots by Naomi, Friedman, Colver and others – who were those kids who paid good money to see better music? God bless 'em; hope they're productive citizens today. It was great to work with them, or see and hear the work they were doing, or even just watch them fly through the air. But I have to say, given the circumstances of my first meeting with Naomi there was always a special kick to running into her and seeing her smile, telling me what she thought of the gig and whether she'd gotten something good that night. I was happy for her, proud of her even.

11. *East*

Here's a bit from Naomi's first letter to me after her move east; it's written on Ras Records stationery:

> "Well, I've finally made the big move. I'm living in Arlington, VA and am workin' here at Ras. So far things have been goin' pretty good – I've been here 16 days now & have been working here a week.... I was able to meet up with Ray [Farrell] on his way back from Russia while he was at Blast First in NY. We met up in Hoboken for the Screaming Trees show then we all drove down to DC for their show here & then they took off back to NYC. The house I'm living at is pretty cool – it's pretty big and the best thing about it is the owner is letting me take a big part of the garage to use as a darkroom which is great. I've been doin' quite a few pix since coming out – I've been doing more photos & going to more gigs in these past 2 weeks than I had in LA for the past 4 or 5 months – nice to be productive again. fIREHOSE were here about 10 days ago – really good to see them again – they didn't know that I had moved so it was a fun surprise.... Last night I went and saw Fugazi, Butterglove, Alter Natives and Burma Jam down in Richmond all of whom were really good. Gwar asked me to do photos of them this Fri. when they come to DC – should be interesting." (NP, May 1, 1989)

Note her listing of each band on the Richmond bill – this level of generous interest is unusual and bands appreciated it. Soon after, on the phone Naomi was almost helpless with laughter as she described applying shoe polish to the sides of Mike Watt's head before that Firehose gig. She said Mike bemoaned his first gray hairs as his "old man gray wings."

Another time on the phone she told me Pettibon had asked her to play Yoko Ono in his Beatles movie, The Holes You Fill. She might have played anybody else, but this American girl was not going to play Yoko!

She told me she said to Raymond, "You're just asking me because I look Asian, right?" I told her she should have done it, but it struck me how quiet she got when relating this. Naomi wanted nothing to come her way because of the Japanese side of her heritage, though this usually just involved swatting away Asian fetishists. In yet another call she told me of being the object of some touring musician's drunken obsession. Said musician, part of D.O.A. mk 3 or 4, thinking she had retired to her bedroom with some other dude, pounded on the door and finally broke it down in a jealous rage. She had instead gone out with friends. She recounted this to me with that same expectant guardedness. I wasn't sure what she expected me to say, but when I mockpled with her, "Naomi, have mercy on those knuckleheads!" she laughed and laughed – practically dropped the phone. I see in her correspondence she added *knucklehead* to her girl-talk put-down terminology: *freak, creep, puker, little boy, old man, bozo*, and in her German period, *arschlecker!* Glad to be of service, Naomi....

I would hear things when old musician friends like Cris Kirkwood, Scott Weinrich, Mike Webber, or Bruce Calderwood seemed to be flirting with death, but they made it through their rough spots more or less in one piece, though I heard that Mike died after heart surgery last November. I probably knew Cris the best of these guys. And these 1994 bits sound just like him, only with an edge of desperation that wasn't there ten years earlier. Cris to David Holthouse:

> "We're not a band; we're nasty little microbes eating away on the skin of this big dumb rotting fruit. We're going to plod along like the Galapagos rock trolls that we are. We'll continue to hawk our wares to the voracious consuming public. Then, a few years after that, death."
> (CK, New Times, July 1994)

Here Cris is asked by Jim Sullivan of the Boston Globe over the phone how touring arenas with the Stone Temple Pilots compares to playing clubs:

> "I'm just so damaged, I can't remember the past. I have nothing to compare it to. You tell me. How was I? How am I? Who am I? Are you my mommy?" (CK, *Ibid.*)

Ray Farrell described Nirvana on tour as a "traveling pharmaceutical circus" and said going out with them changed the Meat Puppets. Ray worked with Nirvana at Geffen and as Cobain respected him he was among those who were part of the intervention intended to break him from drugs. When Ray got to Geffen he found himself in the office next to the boss and David wanted to talk to Ray about SST. Ray writes, "he met J. Mascis and the Puppets separately and wanted to know what their problem was. He tried calling Greg Ginn but did not get a response." (RF, Aug. 8, 2005)

Now the Kirkwood brothers are back together in Austin. Spot's been there for twenty years. Bob Mould may still be there and Davo was last seen there. And now I hear Greg just moved there. Sounds like the makings of a good bar-fight.

I think Reggie Rector is dead, though some suspect not. I called Jack Brewer from Chicago once and interrupted his reconciliation with Reggie, who under the spell of addiction had ripped him off; Jack put Reggie on the phone so I could tell him how good he was and to keep it together and that I was including a Naomi shot of his band, Secret Hate, in my book (1st ed.). He was one of the best guitar players in L.A. (put him in NYC and he blows the Black Rock Coalition to Bayonne) – then suddenly we hear shot dead on the streets of Long Beach, presumably over drug debts. Jack wrote up Reggie's rationale as he knew it for a song on the recent, probably best Saccharine Trust album, "The Great One Is Dead":

> "Self sufficient working mentor
> As sweet as the word please
> These streets are rugged
> And have tolled me back to you again
> I have nothing, nothing have I lost
> But my pride, and now that is yours.
> Set me on your couch, so warm and soft
> My feet will stand again, when they can or must...
>
> I was on a different plateau
> You are just too decent, you would never know...
>
> Man, these streets are for rodents
> And I even owe them"
> (Jack Brewer, "Reggie's Plateau")

Jack is convinced that Reggie faked his death and left town – could that be possible? And never played guitar again?!

I never heard anything like these stories about Naomi. My concern for her had always been about whether any musician could ever commit to her, and in truth whether she could commit back. I suspected her father was the only man who could ever cause her to despair, and I trusted that that would never happen again. And the east coast move and her frequent trips to Europe had rejuvenated her; after arriving on the East Coast she dropped the black and began to dress Cali – board shorts, T-shirts, and Vans!

She'd write from Germany, France, and Italy. She shot touring American bands there and went off to shoot historical sites of interest to her; I've seen impressive color shots she took at Birkenau – pink winter sunsets over the empty, snow-covered, wire-enclosed yards, and trees that seem to shoot obscenely high out of that ground. A friend pointed out that Naomi found the Japanese design elements in the place. She'd read alot about the Nazis, but the death camp seemed to sober her about any price she may have paid racially (see addendum).

Only once on the phone did she seem the slightest bit upset to me. She called in June 1993 after having gone out for her first and perhaps only time as a tour manager – she had booked the tour as well. It was a Saint Vitus/Internal Void tour of the east coast – the T-shirt reads "I Survived the Doom!" Great music of course, a legendary tour even, but a disaster as well. This is from a Blood Farmers interview online, they opened one of the shows:

> "Eli: That tour was hilarious, but very sad at the same time. We spent a long weekend with them. Thursday night we did a gig at this club in Jersey... I think everybody split $20 or something. We were living in a three-bedroom apartment with our friend Lew and his girlfriend and both bands and the crew stayed at our apartment. Something like 16 people! Some army of tough-looking badasses they were. Me and Dave were just these skinny kids who loved metal. They WERE metal. That weekend Dave and I went with them when they had two gigs on the Jersey shore which each had their own little tragedies. The Saturday night gig... had some sort of screwing of Vitus that I don't remember and they were so pissed they only played three songs. The next day was a matinee gig at another dive... I remember JD [I.V.] getting into some kind of beef with the management over something (I think it was about drinking). After they played, the wonderful Naomi Petersen clogged up the sink in the ladies room and left the water running and some fat jerk came outside with a pit bull and was threatening to set it

> loose on us. He was wearing a shirt that said, 'Increase the peace.'" (Eli Brown, Leafhound.com)

Eli had only seen Naomi over the course of those couple days and yet was still struck by her ten years later. She was a grace note in a hard rock world, albeit one that wasn't going to let some scumbag rip off her bands without a protest. This night it would be the New Jersey cops who folded before Naomi; according to Chandler she soon had them shrugging off the complaint and instead telling her Bruce Springsteen stories! I can just picture her feigned, yet warm, enthusiastic interest. I imagine the cops remember it too.

    She was something of a legend herself as stories of SST just loomed larger once Black Flag was gone and Nirvana's breakthrough seemed to allow that it had all amounted to something in pop historical terms. In those years SST seemed even to be clothing the musicians of America. I saw Soundgarden at the Cubby Bear and two of them were wearing Saint Vitus shirts (Naomi design), and in many of her later shots players are wearing the shirts of other SST bands. Naomi must've cut some figure on the east coast, as unassuming and unpretentious as she was. Scott Crawford, then of <u>Noiseworks</u> (now editor of <u>Harp</u>) writes:

> "I worked closely with Naomi in the early nineties.... As a hardcore punk junkie who read <u>Flipside</u> and <u>Maximum Rock 'n Roll</u>, I felt like I was working with Annie Leibovitz." (SC, Sept. 19, 2005)

Scott also admits to having had a crush on her – join the club. There are scattered, admiring references to her on the web (often with her last name misspelled), and I'm guessing there were more than a few songs written about her if one could only crack the code. I noticed as I was leaving SST that she was maturing into quite a beautiful woman. I hope she got to overhear people in the know whispering to each other, "Dude, that's Naomi Petersen!" Having spotted her they could rest assured that they were where it was at.

    But this time on the phone she got audibly drunk as we talked. It was as if she had bolted down a fair amount of the hard stuff, then called. She sounded fine at first.

    I remember the one time I ever saw her with a beer in hand instead of her camera because it was so unusual. It was at the Anti-Club in 1984 and we were perhaps sitting out some lesser band, but I had to smile and comment on it – she held the bottle in both hands like it was a small brown bird (she was still underage).

Now on the phone though, she seemed most upset that she had had a falling out with her friends in Saint Vitus. As she drunkenly told it, at some point when the tour had gone terminally wrong she'd been called "a fucking Jap." I know the guys in Saint Vitus well and they are not badasses; they are sweet, earnest dudes unless you try to mess with their sound. I believe rather that she was called "a fucking bitch" – hey, there's a *big* difference in this case! Naomi was not frail, and she was not crying, but it hurt her that she had volunteered to help her friends string together some gigs and then have it fail and feel blamed. Naomi knew the world was often harsh for her musician friends, but she generally operated outside the gory details. Her small lie, if that, tells me that she'd been deeply wounded by those damn Simi girls, and alcohol just encouraged her to poke this wound. I guess she was trying to impress upon me the scale of the betrayal she felt by plugging it into the most painful memories she had. Both Rosetta and Kara stressed to me how vicious they'd found other girls to be. Naomi always had a girlfriend with which to bomb around at night, but the names of those friends change quickly in her calendars. She seemed not to have had any long-term girl friends. And so it shook her when long-term musician friends seemed mad at her.

She'd had her fill of Simi Valley and the eternal now of Los Angeles. She loved that history was visible and accessible around the D.C. area and in Europe. She wrote how she envied Ray Farrell's trip to Moscow with Sonic Youth, and looked forward to going to Australia, and one day moving to Germany, but all this interest in the outside world seemed to stop at Japan. She shared an aesthetic interest in fascist regalia with Jeff Nelson, but his interest ranged as well to the Japanese Imperial Army and he noticed that Naomi seemed to have zero interest in anything to do with her birthplace. (Odd, that in dyeing her hair black she made herself look more purely Japanese, which I suppose argues that punk style did do for Naomi what she required of it.) Remember that she remained a citizen of Japan, for all her apparent disinterest. She wrote me from the east coast that she was adding a waitress job at Benihana's. She thought that was funny, "Can't quite picture it myself but they asked me (I had applied as a cashier)." Can't picture it, Naomi?! True to form the other waitresses, all Japanese-speaking, hated her, probably all the more so since the founder of the restaurant chain thought she was great and remembered her from the in six years. No-one slept on the office floor. No-one approached working fifty hour weeks. And suddenly they'd be off to school or marriage – unbelievable things in SST terms.

And the kids in contemporary audiences couldn't take in the music our bands played; it was too musical, too much to process for kids for whom punk music need only be another lifestyle accoutrement to match hair/clothes/tattoos... I was releasing films on videotape in those years and Bill read the boilerplate videobox copy I wrote for Doug Cawker's rock film, Born to Lose, something about the reality behind the colorful stage lights, and he looked up and said, "I don't think people want to know about what's behind the lights."

Naomi fell in love with the plumber who came to fix her sink. John Harper was also into music. He worked for his family's company near the Ras offices. She married John on August 26, 1998 and went to work at their office. It might have looked as if she'd gotten off the rock and roll merry-go-round in time to make a family for herself – she was only 34. But Jeff and others would still get calls from her and though she would deny she was drinking they suspected otherwise. She complained about her husband. Scott Weinrich had known Naomi since joining Saint Vitus in L.A. But even this badass, with his own struggle to keep his life and music together, would make time for Naomi. He was quite ready to go down there and beat him up if she wanted it done, but at the offer she would pull back. Naomi told her brother Chris that John was unnerved by all the musicians who stayed in touch with her, and he didn't like that she kept her name. But she was proud of the name she'd made for herself. Her husband was not a drinker and became one more person to hide her drinking from. Chris describes John as family-oriented. Naomi was not going to have children. They were soon separated.

Gary heard from her and she sounded fine. He offered to hire her again part-time but then he saw her drunk in daylight hours and had second thoughts. Chris Bopst of the Alter-Natives (now doing radio) remembers,

> "The last time I saw her was probably 3 or so years ago [-01] and she seemed just like her old self. No drugs and very little, if any, drinking. She was in good spirits and we talked about her managing, I think this is correct, Saint Vitus? Everything seemed good with her and we rocked out to, 'Neat, Neat, Neat' by the Damned. She loved the Damned...."
> (CB, May 8, 2005)

Long Beach Benihana's.

In any case I did not remark that night on her increasing slurring of words over the course of the call, but instead assured her that no-one in Saint Vitus, or on earth, hated her and I insisted that she stay out of that end of the music business. I wish I had that call back because I know she wanted something more from me, a purer sympathy that didn't involve making excuses for anyone else. She had revealed her problem to me, but thinking it pegged to a specific disappointment I missed it. I should have called her the next day. I had invited her to Chicago, but she never came, and then I moved to Wyoming, where nobody ever goes.

Perhaps this disappointment forced her to rethink some things. In 1998 Naomi traveled with her family to Japan for a family reunion for the first time since she was 14. And she went back a second time with just her mother. What must the Kashimura family have made of this willful, flamboyant American daughter of the Japanese woman who took a flyer on the American she loved? My guess is they were flattered by the interest of their exotic American relation. However, at 14 while in Japan her mother's concern that Naomi disguise that she was left-handed so as to avoid such loss of face as to be unimaginable, certainly brought home to Naomi just how much a *gaijin* she was. In a photo from the 1998 trip of a traditional dinner with Takeyo's family, Naomi and her father can be seen boldly clutching chopsticks in their left hands, whereas mother and brother seem in harmony with their hosts. Chris tells me that once the family returned to the hotel to turn in for the night, he caught her preparing to go back out alone. He tried to keep her from going, but couldn't.

12. Nineties

Gary Himelfarb of Ras Records had hired Naomi to do his accounts. She shot very few reggae artists although the company was a major nexus for the music in America. I think the music didn't draw her to those gigs. Naomi liked urgency and edge in her music, and she preferred a machismo that was at war with itself in her musicians. In a letter she remarked on the cocksure sexism of visiting Rastas. She went to Jamaica once to help Gary put on the Negril Westend Reggae Fest (Mar. 13-14, 1993). She also did accounts at the 9:30 Club in Washington for a time in the early nineties. Judging by her weekly planner notations for the early nineties she was increasingly at wits end juggling the jobs, the bands, the boys, the night classes, and the partying. (*"Oh man, what a day!"* May 30, 1992; *"LIFE JUST GETTIN' MUCH TOO HECTIC!"* Feb. 8, 1993)

Jack Brewer saw Naomi in the mid-nineties when she had just come out of the hospital for her recurring kidney infection and looked thinner but otherwise fine – in fact, "hot" was his word. Chuck Dukowski saw her in the late nineties and also didn't pick up on any trouble she might be having. Dave Chandler doesn't remember seeing her drink anything harder than beer. The same for most of us.

But in her thirties Naomi seemed to be losing interest or faith in music and musicians. And as she got older her friends toured less and the new bands were getting to be significantly younger than her. Farrell tells me she wanted to cut her ties to the music scene, especially the men. I last called her in 1997 from Laramie; Drag City was reissuing the Nig-Heist album and was looking for photos. Naomi told me those negatives were lost and she seemed disinterested and I felt busted, calling only when I needed something from Naomi-the-photographer. I thought of her again a few years later when Bill Stevenson and I were brainstorming about what adult we might hire to run our record labels; we tried instead to make do with some young kids, and lets just say they don't make them like they used to. We went through four regimes

But her regular lapses began to interfere with working.

Jeff Nelson last saw Naomi at the Iota Club in Arlington in 2001. He was there with a friend but Naomi was hours late. When she did show she was virtually passed out on her feet, though she managed to laugh at Jeff's now balding head. He took her back to her friends' house where she stayed while separated from her husband. She collapsed and Jeff rode with her in an ambulance while the others followed. Jeff then heard about Naomi's problem from her friends Kevin and Katrina while they sat in the waiting room of the hospital.

The episode involved extremely low blood pressure and near liver failure and she was warned that another drunk like that would kill her. Naomi's mother flew out and checked her into a treatment center in Virginia, and then to the Fretwell half-way house.

In letters through the years she worried about whether she was being productive enough with her camera or artwork. She was driven, though not particularly ambitious about her work once done. She never made her own connections with the print media as Glen Friedman had, and when they fell into her lap she was too involved elsewhere to work them for what they might be worth. She never fretted much over who was ripping off her images or misspelling her name. She apparently never gave an interview to any fanzine, never was profiled anywhere... She seems to have been on-line in 2002-3 but if she was in regular email contact with anyone I'm unaware of it.

Her husband visited her at the Fretwell Center at Edgehill in Virginia. In a photo (nearby) John looks as if he was positive and encouraging to her, but he certainly knew there would be no children. A child would require her to live much longer, a liver transplant might mean another thirty years of a life that would be utterly unlike the one she knew and loved. They loved each other but she made promises, broke them and her drinking made him angry and abusive. Chris would get calls from his sister. Once she said nothing, just cried over the phone. John, a big guy anyway, now towers over a shrunken, fragile-looking Naomi. She is 36.

13. *The Ventriloquist's Muse*

Men buzz around as hardly more than hairy boys until the hand of fate squashes them in their tracks like bugs. Women's lives are demarcated by a series of traumatic, usually bloody, rehearsals for death: the death of the little girl at menses, the death of the nymph at the loss of virginity, the death of the single girl at marriage, the death of the bride at the birth of the mother, the death of the mother at menopause. On occasion, under such pressures a girl might easily add some bloodletting of her own.

Naomi's best friends, the musicians, could often barely save themselves from the inchoate demands of their cruel muse; most were playing music less frequently or had moved on to more dependable gigs to support the woman they finally paired up with. The girls she knew had moved beyond their music scene pasts and were now likely the hippie mom-next-door or some kid's eccentric aunt. She had been an insider but now found herself outside.

Our modern American life comes tagged with conceits like individualism, feminism, self-actualization, etc., but in truth we are simply loosed to our own devices; here's your birth control, you already have your free will. The many brave Philosophers, Playboys and Feminists of the post-war era had their ideas about how it was all gonna be. Something else entirely happened.

The world outside the door is harsh on even the best of families, and nowhere harsher than in the Los Angeles of that day. From 1960 to 1973 youth culture bohemia was idealistic and still believed its way past the gathering dangers; thereafter bohemia believed in very little but art and sex and destruction, and things got much darker – dangers were embraced (the ubiquitous Charles Manson and the True Crime hit parade), and then it seemed even art was jettisoned.

The first women affected by the sexual revolution in the midsixties tried to redraft its terms by the early seventies. But it was a numbers game; in his book, How We Got Here – The 70s (*Basic*), David Frum describes how the baby boom had reversed what he calls the earlier " silent mathematical undertow [that] tugged *him* to do things *her* way." Men now had the upper hand and though while in college they used the new youth style to drive off older men, they soon found it advantageous to trade for younger girls themselves. And younger women could never be counted on by that first group of feminists to help enforce some new version of the code they had just obliterated. Joshua Zeitz in his book, Flapper (*Crown*), notes the parallel between the disappointment of the Suffragettes of the 1910s with the Flappers of the 1920s, and that of the seventies feminists with younger women thereafter.

A writer friend of mine of that first sixties cohort responded to Naomi's story with this:

> "Women can't go with the wild ideals of the time because they always have the pain of compromising with reality, given such a short period of time on the biological clock. And yet they have to gamble on the sex thing of their times, the old way or the new way, and either way they never get to discover their own female instinct."
> (Jane Schuman, June 17, 2005)

There were versions of a reconstituted female code, though these were improvised and abused by the girls themselves. And once out of school it was every girl for herself, and with the Pill and liberalized abortion and divorce laws one can easily see how the feminist effort to allow individual women to escape tragic fates had allowed men in general to sink to caddishness – think the Clintons' marriage writ large.

The seventies also saw a male flight from women and a move on younger women and girls; again, demographic numbers were still encouraging this as well. Culturally we saw through Hollywood's lens a pedophiliac reverie on Jodie Foster, Kristy McNichol, Brooke Shields, Linda Blair, Tatum O'Neal... It seemed every male would-be assassin was trying to impress Jodie Foster, while the gun-waving girls were trying to impress Charlie Manson. (They didn't make 'em like Oswald anymore.) And Kim Fowley was serving up one jail-bait fantasy after another: The Runaways, Venus & the Razorblades, Dyan Diamond...

The pop culture machinery today seems most concerned with convincing young girls that they are as horny as guys, and women's studies is lately obsessed with stamping out the very idea there could be a post-abortion syndrome. And the tactical need of the young woman to insist that such are so demands continuation of old school female silence underneath all the latest noise.

PORTFOLIO

Naomi generally shot bands rather than individuals and so her work is overwhelmingly framed horizontally. The design limitations of this book led me to emphasize the best vertical work so as to be able to print them full page.

•Mike Watt, solo, Jan. 22, 1994 - San Pedro

•Milo Aukerman / The Descendents, 1984 - Anti-Club, L.A.

•Saint Vitus, 1983 - Pacific Crest Cemetery, Redondo Beach

•Henry Rollins / Black Flag, 1984 - Global, Redondo Beach

•Guns n' Roses. July 11, 1986 - Troubadour, West L.A.

•Saccharine Trust, July 13, 1982 - Unicorn, Santa Monica

• Dez Cadena / D.C.3, 1985

•Reed Mullin / C.O.C., 1987

•H.R. Paul Hudson / Bad Brains, March. 3, 1988

•Steve McDonald / Redd Kross, 1988

•Screaming Trees. April, 22, 1989 - Maxwell's, Hoboken, NJ
•Nirvana. Apr. 29, 1990 - near 9:30 Club, Washington, D.C.

•Stop on the 'Doom' tour, 1993

•The Obsessed, 1994 - Colorado

•Sonic Youth, 1985 - Hollywood ·

14. In Wonderland

When I first moved to Hollywood in fall 1976 I was amazed at how grimy and grim this sunny, palm-lined place was. Yet you'd drive up into Beverly Hills, UCLA or the Palisades and wonder for a moment if it was okay to be driving there. I spent the first night in my car in the Angeles National Forest northeast of town during a heavy thunderstorm. The next day was the cleanest I ever saw Los Angeles. I got the paper and stopped at the Canterbury to look at an apartment but the lobby was flooded and the janitor mopping it up said the manager was out. I would've got into punk rock a lot sooner if he'd been in. The lay of the city confused me and I wound up going back up to San Francisco where I had relatives and more seriously tried to find an apt and job up there for a few weeks. That didn't come together either, so I went back to L.A. and immediately lucked into a room at Yucca & Wilcox for $90/mo., and a job at the Vogue Theater.

Visibility was typically about six blocks and the sun cooked the haze until it stung your eyes. Pan-handlers stumbled along Hollywood Blvd with barely enough energy to importune you. They'd eat out of the dumpster behind the market on Highland. Energy came from the kids and the immigrants. Armenians and Filipinos raised their kids in cheap apartments right off the Hollywood Walk of Fame, which the skate-kids loved for its smooth, seamless surface. Wallich's Music City looked like a rec-biz time-piece; Music Plus had a life-size Boz Scaggs cutout under Palm tree display (he was four foot tall, right?); I met Larry Fischer at Platterpus; Kris Kristofferson and Barbra Streisand were playing rockers in "A Star Is Born" at the Cinerama Dome; Rhino Records had the soundtrack cover ripped up and nailed to their door in protest over the new list price of 8.98; Led Zeppelin's concert film-with-fantasy-segments boondoggle, "The Song Remains the Same," was on one screen; Swan Song was trying to break Detective on radio but Foreigner won the battle of the retreads, then known as super-groups. Burnt-out Bowie, Bad Company and Aerosmith could be heard coming from the last head shop on the Boulevard. Bowie and Iggy had to leave. So did John Lennon. Plenty more had to leave but didn't. Roman Polanski was arrested in spring of 1977. The new SoCal rock royalty got theirs and moved up into the hills and never came down. Warner Bros. Records was losing its mojo to Casablanca Records. At the movie theater the candy girls – mostly Jewish, Hispanic, or Filipino – were propositioned by one photographer after another. Models were being killed by one of these "photographers." Their bodies were dug up decades later in the Angeles National Forest.

But Los Angeles would be the only place in America where the original sixties/seventies underground impetus (Velvets/Sabbath/Stooges/Dolls/Ramones, *et. al.*) was forced overground intact. Everywhere else the urban underground was reflexively self-quarantined against the kids in the suburbs until opportunities to get signed and get airplay presented themselves. The resulting laundering via the major labels sidetracked that music safely into a proto-college alt-rock, something entirely overground in cultural terms if not always in sales terms – those kids in the suburbs decided that.

But with Los Angeles you had a suburban-looking wonderland of accessible urban attractions, and lower level industry entrepreneurs trying to ride street culture up into media careers, as well as an ambitious, demanding, fractured population of recent arrivals looking restlessly for something new and improved.

The punks were young but dimly conscious that we were tramping over the rich humus of Los Angeles' short past. Exene for one had a look that directly referenced silent era vamps. I went to a lot of movies that first year in Hollywood; I could see first runs for free. But I also went to the many art-houses and repertory cinemas. A favorite was the Picfair, run by Iranians it showed Japanese films. One theater that intrigued me, the Silent Movie Theatre, was all boarded up, but with painted advertising panels touting the glories of the silent era and promising to reopen soon. It did much later and a second closure was a scandalous homosexual murder mystery you can read about online. I only remember seeing one punk rocker that year in L.A. – it was probably Hellin Killer with that orange buzzcut running around the NuArt theater at a midnight showing of "A Clockwork Orange." I also wandered by the flyer-covered corner near the Ivar Theater; it looked closed but was probably one of those other Masques.

Lydia Lunch, ex of New York, said of L.A.:

> I think people have a big misunderstanding of L.A. and a prejudice.... There's so much mystery here, and so many broken hearts and so much disappointment."
> (LL, Neumu.com, 2005)

The Vogue theater was managed by a Greek singing star named George Michaelides. He showed me little color repros of his old albums that he had in his wallet. I don't think he moved to Hollywood to manage a movie theater – his Mediterranean shrug was classic and he found it quite useful in L.A. One night during the late run of Mel Brooks' "Silent Movie," after the box-office and candy-stand were closed and only the projectionist and I were left, several people came out of the auditorium complaining about some disruptive person. Inside someone was scoffing so loudly at what he was seeing up on screen that I had to ask him to leave. He was a thin, old guy. He grabbed his two large shopping bags and muttered angrily as he complied. Out in the lobby, before disappearing down the boulevard, he turned and yelled at me, "I made this town!" I wish I had asked his name.

Jed Perl in his history of the post-war rise of the New York art world, New Art City (*Knopf*), makes much of the accelerating pace of the artist's life in that city as the forties moved through to the sixties. His comparison is with Paris which NYC had just superceded. Don't know what this means but here's one corner of Los Angeles' art world before anyone knew that it had superceded New York:

> "06-29-84 Hermosa Beach CA: Big Friday night. Pettibon is listening to jazz and watching the baseball game. Anything could happen. Anything? Well it's really a big fat zilch. Nothing ever happens around here. Kind of cool in a way. You get time to yourself in this house. No one ever calls. No one comes over. Pettibon never stops working. He rarely talks. He just draws and reads and he never stops. It's incredible. At the end of the day, there is a pile of drawings on the floor." (HR, Get In the Van, 2.13.61)

The music writers of Los Angeles at <u>Slash</u> and <u>No Mag</u> were sophisticated and a bit older but they stayed interested in what the kids were coming up with. The <u>Flipside</u> crew was far less sophisticated but no other fanzine covered a city's live music like its crew did. I had also lived in Chicago, Denver, Portland, and Berkeley through the seventies and I was thrilled to get back to L.A. in 1981, where real things were possible. *Real*, perhaps, because to do real one must be *doing*, rather than posturing or scamming. And to *do*, it helps to be in some ways naïve, young, and open to inspiration. Check out those radio commercials on Black Flag's "Everything Went Black" album; one is struck by how direct was their challenge to just about everyone, and how fun it must have been. In more conventional urban environments sophistication and politics kill that all off.

Maybe one key secret of L.A.'s many was hit on by Chester Himes who into the mouth of one of his great black male characters (Robert Jones) he places the line: "Just between you and me, Los Angeles is the most overrated, lousiest, countriest, phoniest city I've ever been in." The *countriest* city! In 1947's "L.A. Blues" Crown Prince Waterford tags it "a big old country town." If the old Spanish cowtown, and Belarus, and the dustbowl, and the Confederacy have let go of their contributions to the city, the memory of empty, quiet land remains with the much larger recent tributes paid from south of Mexico City, and north of Java.

After I'd decided to move back to L.A. in 1981 I saw Black Flag a couple more times in SF (Aug. 29-30, 1981) and I carefully watched the support bands they brought up as I'd be working with them as well. These were the Minutemen, and Saccharine Trust, of course, but another made a strong impression as well. I had expected Overkill, but they had cancelled and the Stains were opening in their place. The hall was already full and these four East L.A. cholos were setting up and getting puzzled looks from the crowd. Guitarist Robert Becerra was ready first and he strolled his long-haired, cigarette-smoking self to the lip of the stage and appraised the City's audience while throwing off a winding, driving, whammy-barred solo that was equal parts habanero and angel dust. *Nobody* soloed in 1981! Becerra was the major early figure insisting on the relevance of early seventies hard rock to punk rock if only because he hated punk rockers so much. And seeing him taunt the San Franciscans just got me more excited about returning to Los Angeles. Hope Robert's doing alright.

After the SF dates, Mugger drove the van back up, we filled it with my stuff and ran it down to the Redondo Phelan Ave. address, which at the time was full of the SST Electronics stock and parts. Then we went up to SST-Unicorn in West Hollywood.

Back in L.A., it seemed everything but the air had changed. Whereas four years earlier I had gotten into the Ramones and Dictators tunes that KROQ was playing ("Sheena Is a Punk Rocker," and "Science Gone Too Far"), and picked up the first issue of <u>Slash</u> (May 1977), I hadn't really figured out what was happening until I got up to Portland. It had been easy to fit into the micro-scene up there, but as Peter Handel and I turned Renaissance into a national mail order/distribution company with an exclusive Rough Trade agreement, the local bands weren't in the mood to help us take them national or international. They were still wed to the ideal of artist autonomy, and we were just shopkeep hippies. The Wipers, and Neo-Boys were as good as anything anywhere else, and the Ziplocs and Lo-tek were also very good. The prog-weirdos were in the house too: Smegma, F.D.M., and Parasites of the Western World.

    Diane was one of the hippest girls up there; she went down to SF and came back with her boyfriend Bruce who intimidated most of the Portland punks but he'd hang at the store to listen to records and told me he was in a band called Flipper. He wasn't in a hurry to get back there so I figured it for a kind of loose set-up. Rozz Rezabek was another commuter – in SF he'd been in Negative Trend and had pulverized his kneecaps on the tables and floors of the North Beach clubs. I remember the only record he ever bought at Renaissance was the Sleepers EP. He was so stoked to see it and said later he'd played it all day long, so I checked into it more seriously and saw he was right; I still listen to it often.

    Jennifer of the Neo-Boys worked at Renaissance; she had turned me on to the Dangerhouse singles. She went down to L.A. and came back with one leg in a cast. She'd hitched a ride in Hollywood and when the guy tried to abduct her she jumped from the moving car. Jennifer took over my KBOO show.

    Two young kids who hung out at the shop were Jim-Jim and Yolanda. When Jim-Jim's parents committed him I collected customers' signatures on a petition to his parents to let him out. His mom called and they were clearly unable to understand him and he them. I drew cartoons for his fanzine, the <u>Oregon Organism</u>. He was later diagnosed as bi-polar and sang for the Psychedelic Unknowns. The cops rousted him last Sept. in downtown Portland as he walked from his half-way house; he said something to them and they jumped on his ribcage and let him die there on the sidewalk. Jim must've said something *really* good. Yolanda was a short Hispanic girl who had just come to town. She started a band with Diane, or at least they had T-shirts made. A year or two later in Berkeley I saw Diane and she said Yolanda had gone to Chicago and leaned over the El platform and let the train hit her head.

SF bands didn't bother sending us record samples; they didn't behave like the L.A. bands. They were all scamming to get a CETA grant, or on SSI disability like Ricky Williams. Those with money obsessed on trading up apartment-wise. They expected to sell their records at Aquarius and then get signed by some label that would take care of the rest. But one day the Dead Kennedys' manager Chi-Chi called and we set up a Portland gig with another good PDX band, The Fix (July 11, 1979). Jello and East Bay Ray were interested that we were moving the company to the Bay Area. Renaissance became Systematic Record Distribution and they gave us their debut 45 to reissue on what would be Systematic's label, Optional Music. But things were limited in the Bay Area too. The scene, the bands, the attitudes, no pressing plants... and then Rough Trade was never very interested in American music so their U.S. branch couldn't amount to much. So I wasn't going to stay long in the Bay Area either.

If you compare the two important rock scene films, Los Angeles' "Decline of Western Civilization" (1981), and Seattle's "Hype!" (1996) you'll find that both were made by outsiders, and the principals and players had their complaints. A year earlier "The Decline" would've featured the Weirdos, and the Screamers but they'd broken up. The Plugz should've been in it. Darby was drunk when the Germs were filmed, and sober when he saw it so he despaired over the film's impending release and this apparently hastened his end by a couple years as his plan had been to live until 25. Still, "Decline" is **heavy**, and "Hype!" *lighter-than-air*. One film is full of cultural drop-outs making something new, and one full of the new socialized, bright-eyed middle class arteoisie of students, fans, collectors... One film no-one asked for and was made with money intended to bankroll a porn film and barely released city by city, and the other was celebrated at Sundance and rolled out nationwide. (Look for the DVD re-release of "Decline," it may include extra Medea and Spot material, though I've heard they can't find the original negatives.)

Involvement in that era's music cost you something. The Los Angeles scene was more organic and total. Results were better and the costs more. It better served male interests which are obvious and lasting, than female's which are immutable and clocked in. But young women were there paying that price. (Think of the L.A. girl bands: Runaways, Go-Gos, Castration Squad, Sexsick, the Disposals, the Superheroines, Raszebrae... and the bands with two or more girls in them: Germs, Bags, Red Cross, to Damascus... not to mention Exene,

Diane Chai, Kira, et. al.) Judging by behavior and art today it seems to me that men are regressing (boys in fact rarely reach manhood), while women are still evolving under the pressures of new responsibilities and opportunities. Perhaps I should say *bourgie* boys, because certainly working class and rural men are being grounded in the reality of trying to make a life with new competitors overseas and immigrant labor over here, or in military service around the globe. A central tension today is that women and girls outside the home depend increasingly on a civil order that seems under siege from a hysterical boy culture brewing up from videogames, comics, and a fallen pop culture. And smaller families mean an increased likelihood that a boy has no sister and hence no clue.

I think of Naomi as a transition figure. To an extent all women are transition figures which is why we open doors for them, but the arts they now inhabit in greater numbers are no longer the drop-out wilderness they were when young Naomi pulled that door open for herself. Things have gotten quite safe. Girls no longer drop out; they intern their way in groups into the music industry for credit in arts or Amer-ican Studies programs. They network. Art is something to manipulate at arm's length, not to live, not to get on you. Author Caitlin Flanagan teases that Art History is "the greatest of all girl majors." All that waste of money and time in liberal arts programs, film schools, etc. I say dynamite them all, for art's sake. All of this middle class safety, so well-camouflaged by tattoos, piercings, porn vamping, suicide kitsch...

You could see it coming in the eighties. We were largely middle class characters, strictly speaking, but in retrospect I can see that we and American culture itself were still roiled by inherited immigrant, working class currents. This no longer seems true. Kara writes that it's hardest to remember all the college kids who churned through SST at the end. Mugger agreed with Kara, "they were all alike." Students study culture and sub-cultures, but they don't imagine dropping out and creating one for themselves. They don't want to risk or forgo the dream-house they imagine themselves living in with its leather couches, wood flooring, stainless steel kitchen, wall-sized screen... Charlotte Pressler, who was a writer involved with the 70s Cleveland scene (and married to Peter Laughner), wrote "[W]e had been promised the end of the world as children, and we weren't getting it." (England's Dreaming, *St. Martin's*) A <u>N.Y. Times</u> columnist recently noted that not one of his students, born in the late 80s, had ever felt the slightest tinge of fear of nuclear holocaust. When their profs disguise their own weak natures with radical but decadent bluster, students get their corrupt disguised message: It's all been done. And therefore, so it may.

15. Acclimation

When Naomi came into SST bleeding all those years ago, she was devastated by her father's anger. But she did not want to die. She wanted to live. Naomi confided in her brother that from an early age she dreamt recurring dreams of her own death. One was an abstract existential nightmare; the other involved an automobile crash on the way toward some goal. She believed these dreams. She was certain she would not live to be forty. She considered herself too impatient to have children and so couldn't imagine motherhood for herself. These certainties determined how she lived, and made of her a kind of nihilist. Against my memory of her considerate, humane female manner such personal nihilism is something to contemplate indeed...

    I did not really know her, then. And her marriage was an attempt at retirement. She avoided guys who were in love with her. Her biological clock was rather a doomsday clock. She wanted to live but knew she would die. I suppose the brain knows its body and she accepted what it whispered to her as she slept. With time short she apparently began to depend on alcohol in high school to suppress anxiety and steel her resolution to get where she needed to go and then act the way she wanted to be. She had no time to waste, and she did not want to sleep alone.

    One could probably write a history of alcohol and dissolve large chunks of lit, music, art, and film histories in it. Alcohol fueled the twenties' roar; the flappers and their beaus were also referred to as the Gin Generation. Gerald Murphy, the ex-pat socialite of twenties France said of F. Scott and Zelda Fitzgerald:

> "You see, they didn't want ordinary pleasures, they hardly noticed good food or wines, but they did want something to happen." (GM, Zelda, *HarperCollins*)

And as smart and brave as they were, they came to depend on alcohol to allow them to behave as they wished to be and be seen. In Jon Bradshaw's biography of thirties torch singer and sixties civil rights benefactor, Libby Holman, he quotes a letter of hers to the writer Jane Bowles wherein she strangely comforts her friend who finished her life in catatonic schizophrenia, "I too long for my body to overtake my mind." Holman was then 66 and drinking herself to death.

In the sixties other drugs contended, but if they freed the mind they did so by tuning out the world. And that may be more a male prerogative, because it doesn't help a woman make her way through the world of men outside. David Lightbourne is an old friend I first met in 1977 in Portland and as a bandleader (Metropolitan Jug Band) and one of the west coast Rounders (Steve Weber's electric combo w/out Village-bound Peter Stampfel) he was part of the beginning of the modern northwest's hardy drug scene. There were some overdose deaths with pills and heroin but Dave, who has drunk nothing but Coca-Cola since 1950, noted that the drinkers in that 60s/70s music scene were the ones that died young. Gary Sisco tells me of an early eighties hangover epiphany he and Michael Hurley woke up to: "Elwood said, 'Crispo, we're going to have to find a new way to socialize.'" Gary writes that he felt naked on stage while sober, "The way we carried on those days, if I tried to do that now for a week it would kill me graveyard dead, I believe." (GS, March 15, 2007)

As self-authored as Darby Crash was he could not get up on stage sober – the audience, even when full of friends, holds such power. When Jeffrey Lee Pierce (Gun Club, <u>Slash</u>) hit the wall with alcohol and had to stop and begin A.A. meetings, he wrote, "I felt ripped off. I blamed God personally...." (Go Tell the Mountain, 2.13.61) In a recent interview Chan Marshall tells Robert Gordon that what she misses about alcohol is "that feeling of warmth," and "The hardest part (about quitting) is remembering things that I've done on tour, on stage, with friends in hotel rooms, different situations that were just really stupid. That's the hardest part – remembering." (<u>Stop Smiling</u> 2007)

In Naomi's case the average human, average female inhibitions she felt were keeping her back seemed reinforced by her own high expectations, and a racial component. Most young women are on the hunt for one man, and then their world settles into an intensely focused microcosm that can be understood and handled. But the way Naomi lived these issues never settled; they stayed alive and even thrived as she became more attractive and confident... until she hit the wall of age. Not old age, middle age. She confronted her high school tormentors by dying her hair, and she confronted aging by changing how she drank.

By 1988 things at SST had gone sour for her. But she loved those guys and what they'd attempted and accomplished, and what they'd allowed her to contribute. But she was determined to revisit something that bothered her about her initiation with Black Flag. Before leaving Los Angeles in early 1989, perhaps to prove to herself that she was no longer that young girl with but one thing to offer, she made a point of one last go, only this time one-on-one with just the man himself. Does that make sense? In the mind of Naomi, I think it would have bothered her deeply were she to conclude her SST affairs otherwise.

From D.C., she wrote that her father had driven her there over the course of four days. Mr. Petersen had been his daughter's artistic mentor, and had warned her she would never make any money photographing bands and who can blame him now for thinking punk rock killed his daughter? He must think back often on those long days on the road with his daughter, and wish they'd been longer still. He certainly hated leaving his bad girl on the east coast and returning home alone.

As it happened, Naomi Petersen the photographer, shot bands making music in a period when rock and roll was an underground phenomenon, 1981 to 1994 or so. SST and others littered an uncaring media world with music and her work to little effect. But those black and white prints sit in the files of newspapers and magazines or, as publications go digital and all-color, they trade on Ebay and wind up in the collections of those who care about that music and try to put its history together.

In her worst moments late in her life, Naomi, on the phone with Jeff Nelson would threaten to destroy her negatives, an enormous mountain of her work-effort at all those crowded, noisy gigs and later, alone in the quiet of her darkroom. It sometimes must have seemed to her that her musician friends valued her photos of them more than they valued her. But she respected the cumulative historical value of her work and the art that it was, above and beyond its personal meaning to her, and so she was no nihilist. I wouldn't claim we were the most dependable bunch of guys, and as there was no money for rock and roll this time around, all interpersonal failings among us ground pitilessly unlubricated by the good life accoutrements that people picture going along with the rock and roll life. It's quite powerful to read Henry's 2nd edition of Get in the Van, wherein his original tour journal entries re Kira stand in all their condensed, van-caged hostility, but are now put into an appreciative, corrective context in the 2004 afterword. Henry explains, "We were living hard in those days and a lot was asked of us and we weren't always all that kind to each other." (This edition is also the first publication to note Naomi's passing.)

Henry as voice and face of Black Flag walked point for Greg but Greg only fitfully watched his back; this was unforgivable. But Greg walked point for all of us, and as the liabilities piled up on his shoulders and more of the best people money couldn't buy threw in with him, we only fitfully watched his back. This too was unforgivable. But, frankly, none of us were going to make good soldiers. At best we were like the fractious Wild Bunch caught at the close of the frontier. Our closing frontier was the sixties cultural revolution as it died out in the seventies and early eighties. In retrospect the Black Flag/SST story looks like a cultural analogue to the Manson-Weathermen-S.L.A.-Black Panther-Nixon White House-People's Temple endgame – art just had more life in it than crime or politics or religion. We weren't the only cultural analogue, but we were uniquely productive. And there's still been no comprehensive critical assessment of the label, one that would account for such forgotten, never heard gems as the Overkill, or Opal albums, or the deep catalogues of Saint Vitus, Slovenly, and Screaming Trees. So it is still not understood just how potent the label was. One of the more interesting rock genres today is called stoner rock. That branch in large part proceeds from those Saint Vitus albums, and for those people they are the most important SST band. Bill, Henry, Spot and myself have puzzled over Greg's nineties discography but we all still love his playing and that stuff also awaits reassessment, assuming it was ever assessed in the first place.

Again, Greg was no romantic, and I see more clearly now how trapped he felt by the fact that "Black Flag" and "SST" meant so much more to everyone around him than they did to him. Greg took them for granted as simple by-products of his muse-chase, though he did confess in the last Black Flag newsletter of late 85: "Even though I'm not generally one to dwell on sentimentality too much, this tour will most likely bring out a few such feelings in me." He came to music only in his late teens, whereas the rest of us were steeped in the disappointment that came with loving music and bands that could not sustain our critical interest. We'd perhaps only dreamt some band or label could ever be so potent and true as we took Black Flag and SST to be. Greg often acted as if we had stolen both from him. Here are two entries in a contemporaneous timeline by the Last's Joe Nolte:

"Sep 28 1979 – Black Flag rehearse for upcoming album

> recording, Greg Ginn gets frustrated & pissed, Keith & I split to see the Go Go's at the Hong Kong
> Sep 29 1979 – Black Flag are supposed to play 2 parties tonight, in North Redondo & Hollywood. They cancel, as Greg is still depressed from previous evening ('I can't think of a single reason why we should play'). Red Cross rush equipment to the Hollywood party and play instead. Greg will remain depressed for days."
> (JN, Commonthreadpunk.com)

The SST/Global superstructure got bigger and heavier and so his occasional despair deepened. In 1983 Greg considered simply giving up the name Black Flag to Unicorn and the County of Los Angeles and starting over with a new name. That may have been the thing to do, but it seemed unthinkable to most of us at the time. Needless to say no-one could come up with a name half as good as Black Flag.

Within the band itself, the unspoken psychodrama compounded through the full-time daily practice regimen, the no-money, no-food, no-sleep privations on tour or in town. Yet each player in turn – Robo, Biscuits, Dukowski, Stevenson, Kira – each had to be fired when they came up short with Greg, because they would stretch themselves mightily against their very own playing natures hoping to comply and get to stay. They would not quit. And they wept as they went out the door. Who were they? Musicians are partiers; what kind of musician behaves *that* way?

Well, the big money boom that first Elvis, then the Beatles, Stones, and Zeppelin rode and enjoyed, had ended when the Stooges, and New York Dolls showed up expecting success commensurate with their genius. They'd begun their decadence *before* their success, however, and success never came. The Ramones persevered in a strange twilight of fringe-success and functional low-rent decadence. Black Flag was further evolved to withstand failure on any scale and this did not allow for much besides musical dedication.

The first lead guitar star was probably Michael Bloomfield and his discography is largely incoherent and he knew it. At 15 in 1958, he was playing in Hayden Thompson's band north of Chicago and sitting in with Muddy Waters on the south side. Paul Butterfield, another white boy running around the most amazing black music scene going, was a hard-case harp-blowing bandleader just signed to Elektra in 1965 when the A&R man Paul Rothschild was dragged to where Bloomfield's crew were jamming; by the set's end Rothschild had negotiated his joining the Butterfield band. Bloomfield did great stuff with Butterfield but quit when a one-off with Al Kooper, "Super Session," made him a star. His own band Electric Flag was probably too ambitious and on the wrong label, plus he was no hard-case:

> "The reason I couldn't stick it out was there were just too many people, too many personal trips, that I had to be in charge of. If you're gonna lead a band, you either have to completely depersonalize it – they're your sidemen, they can just go die in their spare time, they can go to hell, you don't care what they do – or they're gonna be like a big family to you. But nothing in between. It just can't be that way." (MB, Michael Bloomfield, *Miller Freeman*)

The early conceit of Black Flag/SST was *We don't fire people; if they're into it, they'll do it. If not, let them go; don't try to convince them to stay.* But art is not like that, and things were no longer like the early days when everyone was a beginner and Keith Morris or Ron Reyes might quit on stage in a melodramatic huff. Now when Greg's musical demands grew and he couldn't get someone he was unhappy with to quit, he was violating that early code he and Chuck had devised; the year-long firing of Chuck, then, was probably the most brutal thing I ever witnessed that didn't involve bloodshed or lawyers. Today, Chuck sounds fine; his band, the Chuck Dukowski Sextet, is saxophone-led (Lynn Johnston) and features his wife Laura Norton on vocals, and now their son Milo on guitar.

I didn't want to leave SST until Black Flag was done. I was bummed when upon first arriving I learned that "Damaged" was to go out through Unicorn-MCA but decided to just hang and see what developed. Money I brought with me got the first Minutemen and Saccharine Trust albums pressed, and Boshard at Thermidor paid for the recording of the Meat Puppets first album (the Overkill 45 and Stains LP were already recorded too). But Greg was bumming as early as late 83 when, with the expectation Unicorn would soon be out of the way, we quietly geared up for new Black Flag releases on SST. Greg did not think that SST was good enough for Black Flag. He liked to think that I was hanging around for the easier stuff, turning college radio hipsters onto the Meat Puppets and Hüsker Dü. I considered that an insult. Certainly there was satisfaction to be had in turning the entire college radio sector and then having smart college boys claim that they had made us! What a joke... It often seemed that no-one but us were even conscious! But I expended more ergs per unit sold scheming to better force-foist upon the world Saccharine Trust or Saint Vitus, and getting SST's roiling aesthetic, for all its non-resolving motion, nevertheless fixed foremost in the minds of people otherwise primed to ignore music for fashion.

In early 1984, Bill Stevenson tried to improve the reception between Greg and I. Couldn't be done, really, but it resulted in Greg trying to give SST to me and Mugger in exchange for helping him and Chuck set up a Black Flag label to be called Nixon Records; I told him if Black Flag wasn't on SST then I was out because I would only postpone my writing further for a band as committed as they. I had tried to work with the Wipers, Dead Kennedys, and Flipper – great bands of course! – but there were limits to what one could do for them just as there were limits to what one might do for the others on SST – again, great bands but not ones that would do the touring, spend the money, live the life, so why would I? I had no ambition to be in the record business, *per se*. I was part of that deathspiral of the sixties boom that Simon Reynolds profiles so well in his book, Rip It Up and Start Again (*Faber & Faber*); its chapters recount one nest of cultural extremists after another dedicated to forcing something new out of themselves and onto the music business and society itself (only the UK ed. has the SST chapter). Delusional perhaps, but one misses that heat when such ambition no longer fires the music of young bands.

So things at SST went along as they would. It wasn't ideal but we were able to function and when we ran into each other at the Ginn's or Calimex or at gigs or Global or SST we could almost have fun together. I walked into Global once and Jordan asked, "So Carducci, are you into this whole WASP concept?" Blackie Lawless was an old Hermosa/ Fleetwood hand, and Dave Tarling, who had produced "Nervous Breakdown" and later, "Loose Nut" and "In My Head," had successfully launched WASP into the majors. Around Global, WASP's debut must've been a welcome respite from their steady diet of Dio albums. I paused before answering suspiciously, "Uhhh, I don't know..." Greg laughed so I know he could still appreciate a burlesque of paranoia at that point. Soon, no one laughed at anyone's jokes.

At SST we went from improvising our way through the weekly crises, to knowing what was coming six months on. Until 1984, if Mugger found cash in the mail the chorus went up, "Let's eat." The label's grosses jumped 400% that year, and another 300% in '85. Still, judged by what we intended, we only ever failed. We did all we could do to get our bands on the radio and written about and then out rocking the great unwashed. Ray Farrell sat down at his desk expecting to start calling college radio stations. No, this was SST; he was there to call commercial radio stations. I think Mugger's exact words were, "Fuck college radio." X's debut album, "Los Angeles" (1980), and Black Flag's, "Damaged" (1981), had each sold over 60,000 copies within months in just L.A. through independent shops and chains alike; each album had several tunes in rotation on KROQ. But this L.A. template for selling the music got short-circuited by the Reebok-wearing cokeheads in KROQ's back office by the end of 1982; they fell for what Simon Reynolds refers to as post-punk entryism (Soft Cell, Human League...), and neither X nor Black Flag ever sold records like that again, despite the improvement of sales out beyond L.A. Hair metal (Motley Crue, Ratt...) and speed metal (Metallica, Megadeth...), had started later on independent labels, but after the synthesizer palette-cleansing, they sounded like rock to the major labels and the underground's media moment passed. For a generation, major rock and roll figures like Michael Kowalski, Darby Crash, Ricky Williams, and Will Shatter made their national music press debuts as obituaries.

Early punk often exhibited the spastic energy of someone straining to avoid suffocation. A couple years later and the kids seemed acclimated to the hopeless conditions and made it work with what little oxygen was available. But it tore a lot of great bands apart, most before they even got into a van to play outside their own town, some before they ever recorded. And even Black Flag with its constant membership turmoil was essentially a band moving forward and repairing itself as fast as it was being ripped apart. Bill Stevenson was pressed recently on how and why he left Black Flag (he left or was fired Apr. 27, 1985). There's always some element of pr euphemism in the answers musicians give to such questions, but this is something different:

> "It's just – I don't know exactly, I mean, if you would've been through – You know, it's a wonder any of us are even alive and even speak to each other, to be honest. You know what I mean? Just to have gone through what we went through, and then still be friends on the back end of it, is a pretty tall order. They used to fuckin' burn – Fuck, one time these guys were whipping us with these belts! It's just like – it was a very tough period, and I was too young to be able to sort of assimilate it all in a way that made sense to me. But I learned

so much from those guys about music and just about life and everything; so I respect them all greatly. And for me, it was a real honor to have even shared the same space with any of them." (BS, markprindle.com, Nov. 2003)

Sometime in the late nineties Henry got glasses, a driver's license and a car. He wrote that he drove down to Redondo and Hermosa and checked out the old addresses, trying to put it all straight in his mind. They'd walled off the door to SST-Redondo on Phelan Ave., he said – No ins or outs. I don't think Henry visited the Ginns. I've told him they want him to stop by, but who knows what Greg told him at the end. Henry came through Laramie to speak at the University and wandering through my upstairs maze of rooms, he wanted to know where my bedroom was. He went straight to it and looked in, saw the mattress on the floor surrounded by junk and came out grinning. I'm glad I was able to bring Mr. Ginn by 2.13.61 once on my way out of town – Regis wanted a lift to Vegas!

There is perhaps a billion dollars at stake that keeps the Rolling Stones talking to each other. Perhaps in Black Flag's case a billion dollars would make no difference. Those were the breaks....

I think only Naomi could float over any and all of the burnt bridges formerly connecting us. And I can't think of any one of us who wouldn't trade those photos for that photographer. Like us she was acclimated to the hopelessness and would charge fanzines as little as five dollars to run her shots. But unlike us she was essentially alone. She fronted so well that even her best friends never knew she was in trouble – never knew she drank. She didn't walk point for the Riot Grrls, or women generally. She often had a girlfriend with which to sally forth, but those friendships didn't last, and I don't think she ever set up house with a guy until she retired into her marriage. Her mission was a solo long-range recon patrol behind enemy lines, or maybe "friendly" lines. Just about the worst mission one could pull.

16. Indian Summer

Naomi always struggled with maintaining the day-to-day structure of her life – car, apartment, darkroom, utilities, etc. She never seemed able to squeeze enough money out of her two or three jobs to float her lifestyle. The whirlwind that was her life never seemed more hectic than in the early nineties. Her planner is an artistic masterpiece of colorful, action micro-text. One must read it with a magnifying glass, turning it this way and that to make out each entry. It's amazing her ballpoints even engaged with such short strokes.

   Approaching thirty she attended A.A. and Sobriety Sisters meetings; she was again taking courses (Sociology, Psychology, Criminology) at a community college. She worries about tests but gets A's; I found a paper she wrote in fall, 1993, "The Use and Abuses of Capital Punishment," and it's a notably unfussy, impartial rundown of the reality and politics of same. Her bookshelves were full of true crime and historical horrors; she was no bleeding heart. It was part of her lifelong study of Man and men. She met with the Peace Corps but wouldn't make their minimum two-year commitment. More restaurant work, and one more star-turn in volunteer and paid work at old folks homes – they loved her but didn't manage to change her mind about aging gracefully herself.

   But then you can see it in her journal: She is suddenly deluged with declarations of love or renewed interest from old musician friends from five or ten years earlier. Most of these guys were a bit older than Naomi and perhaps nearing forty and coming off failed serious relationships, finding that their girlfriends had secretly expected that they would finally give up on their music, sell their guitar and start filling out job applications. I imagine them concluding simultaneously from all corners of the country that Naomi was the one girl they'd met who could understand them as they were. A dream-girl. These were guys in sophisto art-bands, primal stoner bands, commercial metal bands, old school punk bands..., musicians who had known her for close to a decade. It dawned on them all that they had never met another girl like Naomi and never would. She laughed at herself as she happily noted all this interest and fretted over the juggling to come: *"I'm so funny!" "What am I doing?! Having fun! Tee hee!" "Life just gettin' much too hectic!"*

After a Guns & Roses/Metallica/Faith No More RFK Stadium concert (July 17, 1992) she notes *"Oh man, Duff so messed up!"* and *"Jim bein' really nice!?"* and *"Pick up Mike and take him to Ras. Hang out w/ Mike, Roddy & Billy. Very nice to see them all again. Kiss Kiss w/ Mike Patton – what a sweetie!! Go home & sleep!"* On January 21, 1994: *"Call James H. OK chat. He sent me a few pictures from X-mas party. YIKES!"* I gather James Hetfield was Naomi's last boyfriend before she met her husband. Naomi told her brother that she'd become an issue between James and Lars. I bet so! As the principal drama in the Metallica documentary, "Some Kind of Monster," is provided by James' sudden decision to enter rehab for alcoholism, we can perhaps imagine various episodes of the James and Naomi show....

She knew her life was absurd and in her prime she enjoyed it immensely. In the twenties she'd have been played by Louise Brooks. But Louise Brooks, like photographer Lee Miller lived a long life; they found a way, reasons. Their issues were complicated as well by alcohol but it didn't kill them so young. Brooks wrote a memoir but regarding it as too candid to be published, burned it. Lee Miller was Man Ray's muse and assistant when they developed the solarization effect that Naomi adapted with partially mixed chemicals for the back of Saint Vitus' "Hallow's Victim" album. Picasso painted Lee Miller six times, once winking at her by placing her photographer's eye at her vagina. And Buñuel reffed that idea in his film, "Viridiana." The point of exposure... The negative... Then, perhaps a positive.

For myself, a writer, the fact that there would be no Naomi memoir was the second thing through my mind at learning she was gone. I'd settle for video of her playing Yoko Ono! But there's apparently nothing like that but for what's in the addendum. She would never be the "smart old witch" that Libby Holman thought the best compensation for one who'd once traded on sex appeal.

Naomi directed her own life so it's no punitive German tale a la "Pandora's Box." Too American for that. (J. Hoberman in his <u>Village Voice</u> review of the recent revival screening describes the French edit of that film where Lulu is found innocent and there is no Jack the Ripper, and the American edit which had Lulu joining the Salvation Army!)

Naomi made occasional motions to write a second act to place between the first and third, but didn't follow through. Past her prime, she seemed to look for someone to take care of her, and yet she had never cultivated such ties to people and escaped those who had tried. I think her husband John came along too late to rescue her. Years earlier (1990) she met Marco Mathieu of the Italian band, Negazione. Marco knew the D.C. music scene and from Italy had long obsessed on things SST and so knew Naomi's name and work years before meeting her. As a European cultural radical he was struck by her love of America and astounded to see the yellow ribbon for the Persian Gulf troops on her door. (Her notes indicate she made music tapes for the troops as well.) Their relationship as charted in her calendar notes was intense and Naomi seems swept up in it and serious about it as they get engaged and travel to meet each other's parents by March, 1991. Marco is a reporter now (La Repubblica) but Naomi remains a vivid memory. When he learned of her death he described feeling as if "a bomb had gone off in his past." There is a missing period in the calendars and when they resume in 1992 Marco has been exiled from her life. The distance contributed, according to Marco, but she never explained and one day began ignoring his letters and phone messages. She seems to have reverted to plan – she'd made her bed and would lie in it. That's a shame because I believe she was still healthy enough in the early nineties to cheat fate and make a future for herself.

Guy Pinhas moved to Los Angeles from Paris to play bass in the Columbia-era Obsessed line-up. He met Naomi on the east coast before a tour of Europe, and she hung with the band for a week of the 1994 Obsessed/Unsane/Entombed tour; there are excellent color slides of the Obsessed at Red Rocks Park in Colorado from this trip, but there were also a number of rolls she never developed, some of which looked good, others looked rather haphazard when I developed them last year – most are heat-damaged. Guy said she was drinking and one night passed out on the bus. He saw her again in L.A. at the end of 1994 when she was out visiting family. Guy saw that Naomi was covered with bruises. "She bruised easily but man, these were some bruises." (Guy Pinhas, Feb. 15, 2007) He was shocked when she said that she would likely marry the guy because he did love her. She didn't want advice and didn't tell Guy who she was talking about.

She was transfixed and burning herself up. She shot Mike Watt, now solo, in January, 1994; the Obsessed tour soon after and then apparently put the camera away. The Obsessed was dropped by

Columbia before a second album and Wino spent a couple lost years in Los Angeles, ultimately returning to Maryland with nothing but the clothes on his back. He got himself together and in early 1997 his new band, Shine, debuted (it soon changed its name to Spirit Caravan). Naomi was there and as far as I can tell it was the last time she used a camera. John Stabb of G.I. wrote to cartoonist Brian Walsby's page:

> "The last time I ran into her was at a MD club called Phantasmagoria where she was seeing Wino's new band Spirit Caravan. She didn't seem too healthy and I felt a bit concerned for her." (JS, myspace.com/walsby, Mar. 19, 2006)

John goes on to mention that his girlfriend felt intimidated by Naomi.

She last wrote to me on March 3, 1997, "I don't go to many gigs anymore – I mostly wind up just being bored." She'd made no plans for this point in her life.

17. Demand

For groupies, just basking in proximity to the display of rock and roll roosters seems enough, as long as they're signed to a major label. Naomi, however, identified strongly with the kind of existential, rejectionist shout typical of the more serious hard rock forms. It's what she needed musicians for. She seemed to share nothing of the style personally, but felt it deeply nonetheless. When she made me cassettes of bands she felt I should know, they would be of such heavy, resounding dread-bombs as Unorthodox, Internal Void, and Dead World. She also loved comedy in a way few women do; she shared this too with us.

Pettibon draws a recurring character (taken from Felix the Cat) that emits an enormous shout of "Va-Voom!" against the landscape. Raymond explains, "He was usually misunderstood by the villagers... With their common everyday speech it was hard for them to relate to such an elementary voice... and by the end of the cartoon he would use his voice to save the village." (Kunsthalle Bern catalog, 1995) In our free, fallen nation this shout is absurd and cannot save the village. Naomi knew her village, her family, was safe whatever lay ahead for her. In the music Naomi favored, the absurd shout's importance was that it maintained something like personal honor in the face of the implacable, inhuman rotation of days, revolution of years, and the hurtling through eternity... in the face of absurd Death that mocks Life. Something like this is a conceit of many young artists as long as the body seems to bounce back from anything, ready for more. Naomi was surely frightened as her body began to hurt and fail, but she just wasn't afraid enough...

However, Naomi, you did will yourself a photographer, *the* music photographer of your era based on the evidence. None other produced the deep coverage of bands high and low that you did on both coasts and elsewhere, and with a noticeable lack of the lightweight, industry foists that most other photographers and media people ran to. Chris D. thought Naomi captured his band the Divine Horsemen best and thought her eye operated with "an intuition untouched by affectation." As with Spot in his production work, it was easy to underestimate Naomi as she did not remake or force bands into some trademark mold – one that would call attention to the stylistic sophistication of the mediator. The unmediated truth of that music is forever accessible for Naomi and Spot having been so selflessly, enthusiastically there as insiders.

Her photos were often seen in less than optimum settings so I think even those familiar with them will be amazed when they see them collected and presented as themselves. I don't pretend to be doing that here. This online response to the first version of this essay communicates well how her work was first seen and what it meant then:

> "If her name rings a bell, but you are having trouble placing it, she was the photographer for SST Records. She took all those tiny photos I'd stare at in fanzines and album jackets when I was a teen. I'd try to discern something about the people who made this frayed and life-changing music; they all looked so ordinary. I remember hearing *Zen Arcade*... and thinking these must be some tough looking guys. And then, a few weeks later, I saw my first Hüsker Dü gig. The audience was all spikes and leather but the guys on stage couldn't be more ordinary. Or loud. Greg Norton's handlebar moustache was totally confounding."
> (Bendy, Jan. 8, 2006, blackstrap.org)

Chris Petersen tells of mentioning to his sister whenever he'd hear some band that she had once talked about – she would have long lost interest. Naomi was happy for friends who scored platinum or got signed to a major label, but what she listened to and photographed was elsewhere. Farrell, while at Geffen, tried to set her up with paid sessions to shoot the heavy hitters but she didn't follow through – she had already shot those bands as they started in small clubs and couldn't make herself interested.

Talking with Jeff Nelson, I mentioned I might offer her family money to strike new prints from her negatives so that in publishing a collection we could be sure none of her best work would go unseen. Jeff smiled at my naiveté regarding the size of her negative cache; he had seen it threatening to fill a bedroom. But of course, Naomi! You were naturally, totally SST about your thing... I apologize for even now underestimating you. I can see the size of the job now, even given the

The radical, hard-working boys from SST Records: Joe Carducci, left, Chuck Dukowski, Mugger and Gregg Ginn.

But the label's troubles were not over: Following the November, cord Husker Du and Minutemen packages cost $3,200 and $1,500

•John Macias, Greg Graffin, 1982. (Jennifer Precious Finch / shockersite.com)
•L.A. Times, Nov. 11, 1984, Troccoli was trying to get us to smile.

BIG GIG WITH THESE BANDS ON JUNE 2 AT THE MUSIC MACHINE!

minutemen, secret hate, nip drivers, slovenly

New Alliance blow-out news:

OUT NOW!

SECRET HATE 'vegetables dancing' (NAR-016) this seven song 12" 45 rpm keg of blast-off shit and pure flame provide the ball-wrenching for the for the time you have in the meantime. Four piece band with THEIR sound and TUNES. Up front sounds from singer, bass, guitar, and drums. Their houses are in Long Beach. There is good jam and blow-out around their riff. Phrases used are 'like it is'. New album being recorded shortly called PANIC STREET. This is a real sound with a band. Not robot-punk. Real.

NIP DRIVERS 'destroy whitey' (NAR-018) this time it's 9 songs on a 12" 45 rpm boom-tube. this band is what is in its own interpretation of what it's saying, and in particular, the way in which the good laughs are spooned out is in short: first place. They are the good flame. Fun is, and at every other instance, what can be and will? Two moments in which the then can be said to be heard. Or what? Like 'house and purple cow', to point out the exactness of it. Sound is sort of similar to the DESCENDENTS. Singing and jokes are sort of different.

MINUTEMEN 'the politics of time' (NAR-017) 27 songs on an LP. Songs that were never recorded except for the cassette tape originals these were had from. That's only 16 of them. The others are studio songs never used on records or used on non-new alliance compilations (and re-mixed besides to make them kick way more butt). And besides those seven are 3 live songs, one from the mojave desert and then one song 'Party With Me Punker' that was recorded at our old practice place with a 4-track like the Urinals used (a urinal song is also included).

SLOVENLY 'even so' (NAR-019) there's 4 songs on this 12" 45 rpm record that we like to call 'd. boon's baby'. Sound is sort of hardcore-boingo with joy division low tone singing (you will notice this but not embarrased for it). One song sings 'south bay' in it and makes me think of Pedro (where I live) when I hear it. Other tunes use abbreviation with both words and whole ideas along with a one-line generalization of the whole of life. They offer you the choice of 'picking for yourself' the one splintered piece of meaning/song-line to base a whole new pillow-head world of non-deal.

All 4 of these bands contain genuine garage-band musicians. They are not trendy-punk. They would barely be here if it wasn't for punk, but this has nothing to do with them coping a pose - like punk, 60's psychedelic, rockabilly, mod, metal or dressing up like mom or dad. This is free expression as it happens in the now - 1984. Try this shit out, check them out, decide whether you want to call them assholes. They leave this part for you.

New Alliance Records - p. o. box 21, san pedro, CA 90733

CENTRAL INTELLIGENCE AGENCY

LANGLEY, VIRGINIA

carducci
sst
p.o. box 1
lawndale, ca. 90602

THE WHITE HOUSE

Mr. Joe Carducci
SST Records
Post Office Box 1
Lawndale, California 90260

•Now it can be told: One big psy-op.

•Suzi Gardner, Spahn ranch infrared b-roll, 1985.
•Henry Rollins, infrared, behind the Ginn's, Hermosa Beach, 1985.
•Jeff Nelson, trip to NYC, 1985.
(all NP)

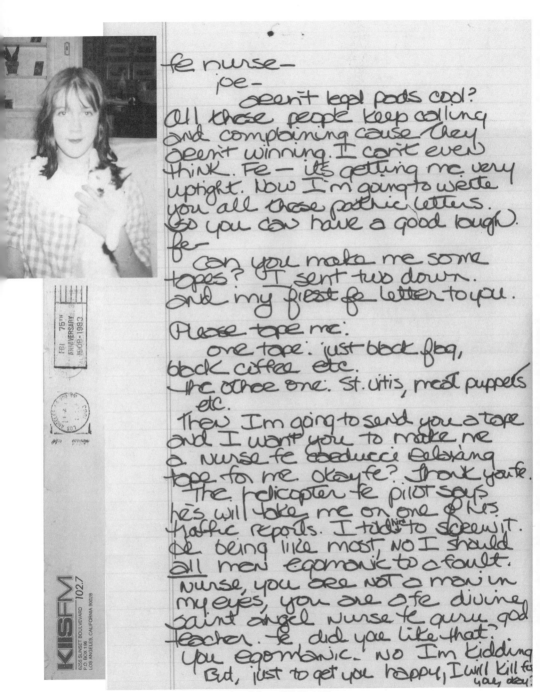

fe nurse—
joe—
aren't legal pads cool?
All these people keep calling
and complaining cause they
aren't winning. I can't even
think. Fe— it's getting me very
uptight. Now I'm going to write
you all these pathetic letters.
So you can have a good laugh.
fe—
Can you make me some
tapes? I sent two down.
and my first fe letter to you.

Please tape me:
 one tape: just black flag,
black coffee etc.
 the other one: St. Vitus, meat puppets
 etc.
Then I'm going to send you a tape
and I want you to make me
a nurse fe Carducci relaxing
tape for me. okay fe? Thank you fe.
 The helicopter fe pilot says
he's will take me on one of his
traffic reports. I told hire to screw it.
de being like most, NO I should
all men egomaniac to a fault.
Nurse, you are NOT a man in
my eyes, you are a fe divine
saint angel nurse fe guru god
teacher. fe did you like that?
you egomaniac. NO I'm kidding
But, just to get you happy, I will kill for
 you dear.

•Letter from Kelley at KIIS-FM, 1983.
•Kelley & Juju, Sherman Oaks, 1984.

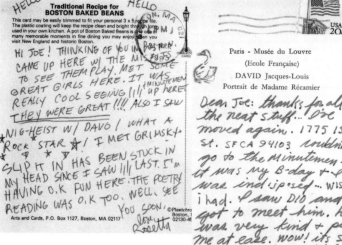

- From Rosetta in Boston and San Francisco.
- Rosetta, 1991, Georgia. (Josh Mason)
- Note left at SST by Rosetta & Teresa, 1983.

•Troccoli & Davo under the truck, 1984. (DRL)
•The Rat Sound rig, Black Flag check, 1984. (DRL)
•Davo & Dave Rat on the truck, 1986. (Phil Newman)

ENTERTAINMENT is designed to gloss over real problems, AND very often those who profess dissent, only add to the deception. WORDS ARE BANDED, but ALWAYS At the whim of the puppeteer. Actionless sloagaNeering is Just Another Punch AND Judy Show. Will Achieve Nothing but the Strengthening of the Status quo. Punk has spawNED Another Rock- AND-Roll Elite, Cheap Rotten Vicious imitations thinking they'll change their world. With dyed hair AND Predictable gestures. Nouveau WANKERS. There's a thousand empty stages waiting for their empty performances, A thousand empty FACES waiting for their Empty STANCES. How MANY timES must we hear rehashed versions, By JERKS whose only Fuck off to the System has been ONE of the wrist? It's the feeding of the 5 Knuckle Shuffle. We might have BEEN A PART of it rather than APART From it!

#121984 CR@SS

BLACK FLAG
P.O. Box 1
LAWNDALE, CALIFORNIA
90260

11/7/85

Mugger, Joe, Ray, et al...

This is me: big toy soldier on tour. Have not ate meat all tour; D. fell off the chuck wagon on the second day. — love, Mike

SST
P.O. Box 1
Lawndale, CA
90260

Hi Joe —

I'm here w/ the Sonics. Most of the audiences want the Sex Pistols. Opening acts are hilarious. Bureaucracy makes a puzzle out of everything. If you solve it, you may proceed. I wonder if you'll actually get this. Hell, its a free country.

Joe Carducci
1640 W Pierce Ave
Chicago IL 60622
USA

•Crass directive, 1985.
•Mike Watt near the Minutemen's end, 1985.
•Ray Farrell in the U.S.S.R., 1989.

•Lisa Carducci, Aug. 1985 in friend's wedding party, a month before her death; the official portrait, and a b-roll image.

P.O. BOX 1 LAWNDALE, CA 90260 U.S.A.
OFFICE: (213) 676-0110

-------PRESS RELEASE--------

12-24-85

We regret to inform you that Dennes Dale Boon (D. Boon) singer guitarist and founding member of San Pedro's MINUTEMEN was killed in an automobile accident in Arizona late Sunday night or early Monday morning December 22, 1985. D. Boon was born in Napa California on April 1, 1958, was a lifetime resident of San Pedro, and graduated from San Pedro High. This is all the information available to us at this time. Ray Farrell can be contacted for additional information.

•D. Boon death release, by Mugger, 1985.

large chunks of priceless material she lost along the way. Thank God for computers and negative scanners.

This SST ethic, as it now seems to be called in the literature, was sourced in the teenage interplay of brothers Greg Ginn and Raymond Pettibon within their household of three brothers, two sisters and their parents. Raymond told the New York Times:

> "We were all kind of in our own world at home. My father was a Republican, like most people in Hermosa Beach, but he wasn't uptight. His politics weren't hippie, but his lifestyle sort of was."

And about Greg...

> "We weren't co-conspirators or anything. But there was a certain shared attitude. Greg had the idea that he could do things for himself. He was a genius."
> (RP, New York Times Magazine, Oct. 9, 2005)

The Times' art critic, Michael Kimmelman got Greg wrong in the piece, but about Greg you will be wrong. Greg stopped talking to Raymond long before the artworld knew the name Pettibon, and that's just *talking*. *Communicating*? Probably not since the end of the seventies. More than once I was reading Mrs. G's Christian Science Monitor while Raymond worked – baseball or basketball on the TV – and Greg would come in and to make conversation ask his brother the score even though he hadn't then followed sports since he picked up the guitar. But I thought I could hear an echo from back when it probably mattered a lot to both of them how the Angels were doing.

Raymond adopted the nickname his father gave him, whereas no-one but Mr. Ginn, and occasionally Mugger, ever called Greg by his: Kierkegaard. The bookstore in Hermosa Beach was named for Either/Or, and he was a key step from within faith toward the enlightenment: "Subjectivity is the truth." His delineations are subtler than that sounds, but then so is Greg's guitar playing. The youngest brother, the bitterly funny Adrian, is a contractor and his father occasionally referred to him as "Cog." Raymond and Greg haven't spoken to each other in twenty years, not even at their father's funeral. This silence is Greg's choice and not just for his brother, and it shoots a peculiar energy through any conversation SST/Black Flag veterans have with each other. This grounds any mere nostalgia in Tragedy – one more reason to thank Greg, I suppose. I hope he's okay.

This calls to mind something Zelda Fitzgerald wrote upon the death of her husband in 1940. She claimed each generation yielded to the "thematic persuasions" of its day:

> "The meter being waltz time which moves nostalgic twilights to their rendezvous, the world believes again in sentiment and turns to fairy tale; whereas those years haunted by the more aggressive sadnesses of march time produce a more dynamic, tragic spiritual compensation."
> (Zelda Fitzgerald, *Collier*)

She thought that her husband's first novels (This Side of Paradise, The Beautiful and Damned), which were of and about that moment, "have been able to defend themselves with a better-perfected hardihood and by means of a faith in *technique* from the heartbreak and subsequent ruthless purpose of the 1920s." Those novels failed in their day, and The Great Gatsby sold even less. The "Damaged" album sold twice as much! And still failed. But it too has defended itself, from fairy tales and ruthless purpose.

I walked into the Ginn house one afternoon in 1983 and Raymond was in his chair turning written ideas into a pile of new drawings and Mrs. G commented to me in her Estonian accent, "Ray is really working hard today." And Raymond – graduated UCLA in economics at nineteen – shrugged and said, "Demand." He even made himself laugh that time.

18. Coherency Cycle

I was not exactly the social director at SST; I saw the gigs, grabbed the first ride back to the south bay and went to sleep so as to get up early, get the papers read over coffee and get on with the task at hand, and be free to shoot baskets by four, shower, and then, unless Mr. Ginn, D. Boon, or Byron Coley had come by with food, walk to the Ginns' to eat something. I did not know much about who was doing what with whom. We were all in thrall to a kind of anarchist personal autonomy as well, which made things that much harder on the girls.

I was trying to learn something about art in the world, while working to mature as a writer. I was always looking beyond my involvement with music; turns out Mugger was too. But we were surrounded by people fully, dangerously committed to music as life. Davo wrote from Global-Redondo to the thousands on the mailing list,

> "At this point in the newsletter, I'd like to cut with the information and try my hand at intimation. I find it real difficult to keep from exaggerating as to how I feel about the people in the Black Flag 'family' and what it is we do because we do so much that my brain never gets a chance to run it all through the coherency cycle. Music and the people who make it are two of the most important things in my world and when I look to express what that means, words don't seem to work for me too well and that in turn only makes those people and their music more precious and my life more meaningful than I am able to grasp." (DC, Summer 1984)

Davo was no longer the uptight twenty year old afraid he'd follow his best childhood friend into the mental hospital; he was now the driver/soundman/roadie/all purpose ice-breaker for the Greatest Show on Earth. Today it's not clear where he is.

By 1984 Black Flag and SST were no longer one world, though certainly still sister planets. Black Flag and its new touring troop were now tethered to Global rather than SST. I didn't hear the tour stories unless there were breakdowns or arrests involved. I learned more from the books by Henry, Joe Cole, and James Parker, and Dave Markey's documentary; Dave went out on the last Black Flag tour with his band, Painted Willie, and a super8 camera. What footage I've seen includes this gem from an exhausted and well beyond frustrated Dave 'Rat Man' Levine, who built the PA and did sound,

> "There comes a point in everyone's life when all the chips are down and the shit keeps fucking up, and you just gotta say: What the fuck... What the fuck... It doesn't matter anymore, you just gotta fucking power... through... the shit."
> (DRL, "Reality 86'd" 1986)

From Joe Cole's book one can deduce that the day that made Ratman spake thus was January 20, 1986 in Baton Rouge,

> "Yesterday was a hellish day for Ratman and I. We had to get a new cylinder head for his truck in the morning, then go to the American Legion Hall and load-in for that evening's show. Then we spent the next eight hours replacing the old cylinder head with the new one only to find that it wouldn't work.... So this morning we rented a Ryder, loaded it up and headed for New Orleans." (JC, Planet Joe, 2.13.61)

Cole on tour was the Waste Master General; he considered Davo "a true road warrior" and often Davo had the first truck with Greg and the others miles ahead of the PA truck Joe often drove with Ratman and Henry:

> "5.11.86 Fayetteville AR: As we pulled into town we passed a group of people demonstrating for anti abortion and Rollins stuck his head out the window and yelled at the crowd, 'Chop 'em up and suck em out. Heil Hitler!' and gave them a Hitler salute...." (JC, Ibid.)

A few weeks later Joe tells a truly insane narrative of the drive from Utah to Denver on acid with Ratman and being pulled over by the Highway Patrol. Cole is full of bad vibes and Ratman has become convinced he's evil and leaves the truck to tell the cops so. The cop leaves Ratman for Cole,

> "'Your friend says you're evil, is that true?' 'No sir, I'm not

evil.'... He took his glasses off and nodded at me. Then he
picked up a packet of birth control pills that Ratman's
girlfriend left on the dashboard. Rollins had drawn
swastikas on the pills and wrote 'Fuck Kill Fuck Kill' all over
the packet. He looked at it for a few seconds and then asked,
'What is this?' (JC, *Ibid.*)

Joe is acquitted of being evil and they proceed to the gig in Denver. Ratman does not exactly authenticate this story. Cole hung around Global because he couldn't get enough of Greg's guitar playing. I don't believe I met him until the Rollins Band's first tour; I introduced myself to him outside of Medusa's in Chicago (May 24, 1987). In his entry for that date he writes of the bad vibe the night before in Detroit and seeing old Black Flag tour graffiti, "Joe Cole's Nightmare Lives on." But it didn't live on long enough. Joe was shot to death resisting a robbery in Dec. 1991; Henry believes Joe saved his life that night. That would've been his instinct after all that tour duty.

It surprised me how affected I was by the news Naomi had died, and that I found out two years after the fact merely by chance in an email from Tim Adams of Ajax Records. He had heard it from Slovenly who had heard the word going around at the San Pedro premiere of the Minutemen doc, "We Jam Econo." I had just heard about Mr. Ginn's passing, but that was within two days of his death. Was Naomi really that forgotten?! That seemed somehow darker to me than the fact itself.

But no... I found out quickly that she was hardly forgotten as I in turn spread the news with my questions. No-one seemed to have any answers but they sure remembered her. (When I wrote Mugger that Mr. Ginn had died, he marveled at how good he'd been to us. A couple months later I wrote him about Naomi. He took a week to respond: "I keep thinking about her, and that I was not that kind to her." That *word* again.) Should I have pushed her and her camera out the door back in 1982, instead of pulling her more deeply into the music world? Might she have finished high school, gone to college, married, taken pictures only of her kids? No... Afraid not. Naomi knew what she was doing, and her father surely had tried everything before he tried the tough love that sent her crash-landing at SST that night years ago.

When D. Boon died in a van rollover just before Christmas 1985 it was just two months after the death by cancer of my sister Lisa. D. was one of the few at SST who knew; he'd lost his mother to cancer and so was sensitive to it. When she was eight Lisa began to grind her teeth in her sleep; the one time I was awake to hear it from down the hall it sounded so loud as to seem superhuman. A little girl could never produce that sound while awake. Sleep is not as easy as it looks. When first diagnosed she wrote in her diary regarding the prospect of dying of cancer, "Nothing that dramatic would ever happen to me." She was in remission for a couple years so I didn't understand what my mother was telling me on the phone, and things were cranking at SST – I felt I was just getting the hang of the job in late 1985 and we finally had the money to do things right. My sister Geri called back the next day and laid it out to me. The tumor was crushing Lisa's lungs. I got there fifteen minutes late. I'm not sure how my parents, doctor and nurse, were able to watch her suffocate.

Lisa's death got me thinking again about leaving SST. After Christmas, Mr. Ginn picked me up at the Long Beach airport and asked me if I was back for the funeral. I laughed, thinking he meant the long-threatened grand SST inhumation when we would all – Black Flag, all ex-members, all suspected future members, the SST and Global crews, the SST bands, the New Alliance bands, Rat Sound, the kids on the mailing list, the entire Ginn clan, the Estonian side if they could be got at, every band Greg ever signed, Spot ever recorded, Naomi ever shot, and all the girls who ever sucked or fucked or winked and walked away – every last one of us pushed into a gargantuan hole in the earth and filled in by bulldozers driven by Jan Wenner and Darryl Gates – silenced once and for all. I thought Regis meant *that* funeral! Mugger hadn't wanted to tell me about D. over the phone during Christmas. But as good a friend as D. was – I still remember his phone number – I felt nothing after what I'd just been through with family. I felt for Jeannine, now wheel-chair bound, and Linda, because I could see them and the challenges ahead for them. But I was left wondering what I really made of these friends or associates or enemies.

I did not charge Naomi a toll back then, which would've been the normal rec-biz practice. An empty gesture, considering, but I hoped she appreciated it. But for throwing in and doing that work under those circumstances I hope to help see her material published in the way it deserves for both its artistic and historical value. With our run-and-gun m.o. at SST we could not afford an art department, and turning records fast to hit the stores before the tours did not allow do-overs when I or the coke-heads at Quadra-color (nice guys all!) fucked it up. Naomi's art might have been better served; I owe her for that.

19. Immer Simi

The Petersens retired to Shell Beach, near Pismo. Leroy now was able to focus on his ceramics work. Chris had moved to Henderson, Nevada to be near his ex-girlfriend and their daughter, Chelsea.

Chris had flown out to D.C. several times on short notice to help Naomi; sometimes he felt he had to fly in without telling her to force help on her. She wouldn't give up on her marriage. After another bad hospitalization around Thanksgiving, 2001, Takeyo went to D.C. for six weeks until Chris could arrive, rent a U-haul and move them and all her stuff to Henderson. Naomi stayed with her parents at Shell Beach. There she attended A.A. meetings, got on the national waiting list for a liver transplant, and considered a divorce but her husband dissuaded her. She did love him, and hoped to get healthy and return to him. But Naomi would not, could not stay sober for longer than three weeks no matter how closely her parents watched her. They purge you from the list for that, the bastards...

Naomi perhaps appreciated the encouragement she got from her family, and friends like Jeff and Henry as she would a warm breeze, but otherwise ignored it. Chris believes that being back home, "made her feel emotionally weak... like she was a teenager again with rules and constant supervision."

Jeff got a Christmas card from her where she wrote, "Glad to be able to tell you I'm back on track and have a part-time job." She was saving up to return to the east coast and thanked him for being "such a good friend." Dave Chandler talked to her in spring 2003 to invite her to their Chicago tune-up for their Wino-era Saint Vitus reunion in Europe. (He invited me too; would that we had both gone.) Dave said Naomi sounded her usual self on the phone but by then wasn't working so didn't have the money to come; she also mentioned she'd had a hysterectomy and was going in for a mammography.

Naomi walked away from one head-on collision and other sleep-deprived, alcohol-related car accidents, as if conceding nothing, or trying to summon her nightmare out into the daylight. Chris writes:

> "I remember driving as fast as I could to Kaiser Hospital in Woodland Hills and trying to prevent her from opening her passenger car door as we were racing down the 101 freeway. She wasn't aware of where we were or what we were doing, as her blood pressure dropped dangerously low. We arrived just in time for her to receive treatment and get stabilized." (CP, March 26, 2007)

Naomi and her mother drove out to Henderson to attend Chelsea's middle school graduation in May 2003. On past family get-togethers Naomi would come into her niece's life like an instant vacation; they'd hit the roller coaster at Knott's Berry Farm without fail. Chelsea says she was too young then to understand why the roller coaster rides had to end. Naomi's bruises now were something different. She took a photo of one on her leg as if she herself was fascinated with how they'd changed. If I understand it, her liver no longer passed any fluid and so rather than drawing in the blood of the bruise, it rose to just under the skin in the form of a large brown patch.

In this year-and-a-half back home, Naomi was reminded what a master ceramicist her father was. Like her he never tended to the marketing of his work and so his profile in that world isn't commensurate with his skill. She asked her father to make her a pot and he made her a pale pink one with pan-Asian features. She then, against her family's wishes, returned east to try to reconcile with her husband. Chris writes:

> "Naomi was a very independent person as you probably know, so it was difficult for her to accept the help that was offered to her. It was hard for us to see her destroy herself like that, but she always had that wry sense of humor and loved to laugh at everything around her, no matter how bad it got." (CP, June 28, 2005)

Brave girl.... On the east coast her attempted reconciliation went badly. After two days John threw her out. Chris again:

> "I was on the phone with her several times throughout the daytime when she was upset.... I arranged for the hotel room that she checked herself into because I didn't want her driving around town aimlessly. I last spoke to her that same afternoon after she checked in and was going to bed early."

(CP, Feb. 10, 2006)

Scott Weinrich found a message on his machine this night but it gave no indication of any desperation. Naomi was to fly back to Los Angeles the next day. Maid service found her that Friday morning, June 13, 2003.

Chris says Naomi's ashes fit perfectly into the pot her father had made for her. Small white crosses line the top, and the bottom reads, "With love to my daughter" and is signed and dated. They are buried in the Simi Valley cemetery. Naomi hated Simi Valley.

20. Us

Los Angeles is my haunted city. I kind of know it, but it's still so alien that my senses are heightened as I drive or walk around in it. In Bruce Caen's novel, Sub-Hollywood, his narrator who is telling his story of those days frets, "Sometimes I think that I am just fantasizing all this because almost none of the architectural structures are the same anymore." He's talking about Hollywood and downtown, but the same is true of the beach and the harbor areas. In Chicago it's clear when you're on a dangerous street. Not so clear in Los Angeles, as the housing is often suburban-looking in the most violent 'hoods. But then there's something *off* about it all too. I think of the gang culture in Los Angeles as an eastern/old world reaction by those who refuse access to the free individualist opportunity the place offers. That opportunity is stark and it will change one, and so many refuse it for their safe place in communal identity.

Like the gangbangers, the city's power elite seems to live in opposition to the city's actual culture,

> "For a swath of America so emblematically cutting-edge as L.A., its serious-minded elites – movers, shakers, journalists – are weirdly, anachronistically old-school."
> (Kurt Andersen, Oct. 30, 2006 New York)

The L.A. Times wanted to be the N.Y. Times and so wound up owned by the Chicago Tribune. Andersen quotes former editor Michael Kinsley, "There's no glory to be the guy who takes the [L.A.] Times local." Do you think the editors ride their new subway to work?

One night in the early 80s I stepped outside someone's house and walked into their small, but thickly planted yard. The sound of a helicopter faded and there was some kind of mist falling – you could feel it rather than see it. It hadn't been a police or news helicopter; they were spraying Malathion. I'd read about it but figured it would take them months to proceed on something that scary. One suddenly had the sense they'd gladly gas the whole lot of us to protect agricultural interests up north from the med-fly. Agriculture wasn't exactly a patchwork of family farms in this state.

I'm a bit on edge in L.A. even when watching Mugger help coach his son's Little League practice in Carson. I look at the kids learn the game and marvel that people are raising their kids here. I read that the aging palms, planted in the twenties are becoming an expensive hazard and so are being replaced through attrition. They aren't native either. A couple years ago while driving in I heard the KROQ morning zoo team imitating Rodney and laughing at his now post-midnight Sunday timeslot and at the station manager's pleas to stop ridiculing Rodney on the air. Then they played some righteous Nickelback. But you can switch to KXLU which Stella runs, or 103.1 where the punks are DJs (Steve Jones, Henry Rollins, Keith Morris...) and you might hear anything. There always was good radio in Los Angeles. The top rated stations are Spanish-language now. I just read in the N.Y. Times that one of these is syndicated in NYC and they're hearing L.A. freeway traffic reports in Manhattan now, in Spanish.

A friend of mine moved from Cleveland to Los Angeles a few years ago and enthusiastically threw himself into some part of what goes on now. We recently emailed back and forth about Arthur, and L.A. Record – both recently back from near-death experiences – and his impressions of L.A.:

> "The things that keep the music alive in L.A. for me right now: The Smell, il Corral, Zamakibo (all three are all-ages clubs), KXLU, totally!, Mag, and Citybeat... with additional support from L.A. Times, Amoeba, Knitting Factory, the Mountain bar, and the Echo. The Cocaine and the Here Here Gallery are also hubs. But mostly it's just interested people planning things, not really any large entities.... The people out here playing music, doing shows and getting excited about things are the most inspiring mutants of all time! They don't ask permissions and they don't really seem to care about anything but keeping going. Needless to say I love L.A.!" (Sean Carney, Dec. 6, 2006)

Sean's made a doc called "40 Bands 80 Minutes!" that captures something of what's going on now. I'd be more likely to check Saccharine Trust at its joints in Silverlake; Mike Watt's are in Santa Monica and San Pedro. I got to see Chuck's family band (and Fatso Jetson) rock the Troubadour last year!

It sounds like the endlessly discussed and planned rehabbing of Hollywood is finally taking. Hollywood & Highland and Hollywood & Vine are being shaped up with big money from downtown and the Westside and made habitable for high-lifes. The Capitol Records parking lot record mart left for Pasadena years ago; Capitol is part of EMI now and the landmark building built with big band-era money was sold for condo housing. Helmi Hisserich of the L.A. Community Redevelopment Agency recently told the <u>N.Y. Times</u>, "It's nice to see that the entertainment industry has taken notice of Hollywood."

On a recent pass through Los Angeles Pettibon told me that Medea had called the house for Greg some twenty-three years after she last barged into SST with her hustler boyfriend demanding song royalties. She had been making threats so Chuck left Spot his gun before Black Flag went on tour. Spot was then splitting an apartment with Dave Van Heusen up in Los Feliz, and recording the Subhumans album at Unicorn. Medea and Lenny would lay in the fold-out sofabed that Greg slept on but never opened because when open it cut the small office in half. When I mentioned Medea to Rosetta recently she copied a letter Davo had written her in this period:

> "Hi Rosetta:
> I'm at Spot's house dropping off some $$ so he can eat. SST owes Spot a lot of money. Got a letter from you today....
>
> I am now at Stoughton Printing way out in Industry (the actual name of this city)! This would be a cool place to live if I was in a heavy metal band.
>
> I had another fucked night last night but I don't want to whine about it, I'll just recap the highlights. The Partiers (R.C.) made a mess of SST. Medea dropped Lenny's TV & broke it. Lenny started to beat the shit out of Medea but she locked herself in the bathroom. To top it all off, someone else has moved into SST for a week. He's the manager of the Subhumans. I spend a lot of time under my table trying to do homework and ignore everybody.
>
> I am now at Edwards Container in Watts! This place is cool. Hank & I came up here once & drove around because he was homesick. D.C. is a lot like Watts. There's isn't one wall that doesn't have something cool spray painted on it. The wall I'm reading now belongs to a gang called The Dirts.
>
> Well – I'm back at SST where I have just completed the massive job of cleaning this place up. It took two hours but at least this place is livable again!! Medea & Lenny bailed with Steve & Jeff (R.C.) for a while so it was cool. When

•At SST-LB 1, 1987: Mugger, Ray Farrell, Raenie, Rich Ford, Craig Ibarra. (Raenie Kane; RK by Walter)

•Jordan Schwartz at SST-LB 1, circa 1987. (NP, I think)
•Davo & Kara with Cris Kirkwood, Phoenix, 1987. (Derrick Bostrom)
•Naomi's early paintings above her SST-LB 1 desk,1987. (NP)

Jeannine G.
555 W. Bonita
San Pedro, CA
90731

Joe Carducci
1640 W. Pierce
Chicago, IL
60622

Dear Joe, It's really good to hear from you. I am really surprised, well not that surprised, to hear about you fixing up a house and becoming, yes, a landlord. I can just picture it.

Well me myself is back in Pedro. Not to protect my name though, it was the best place for the money and I could actually get in to the bathroom. It's kind of funny though, I am about four houses up from George H. just a few blocks from where I lived on Santa Cruz.

As for working, nothing yet. I've just been trying to get use to taking care of myself, but I think I'm just about ready. (Slowly but Surely!)

I don't know if you've heard but my sister is now living in Albequerque, she's working and going to school, she's living with her uncle George, her address is
1619 Girar Dr. S.E.
Albequerque, NM 87106
Will take care, keep Warm, and Be Good!!

Have A
Merry Christmas
And A Happy
New Year.

Love Ya, Jeannine G.

• Christmas card from Jeannine, 1987.
• Jeannine, 1991 (Elise Thompson).

• Word from the road: Davo on Meat Puppets 1987 European tour. Mike Watt on Firehose 1988 tour. Mark Hosler of Negativland lost in Wales, 1989. (courtesy RK)

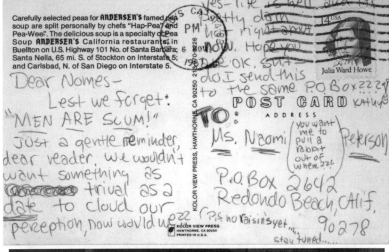

- Word from Kathy at Stuart Anderson's Nov. 6, 1987.
- Farewell Party for Naomi the night before she left L.A., Apr. 8, 1989, McGee's Long Beach.
- Naomi at Benihana's, D.C. area, 1989.
- Dio talisman found among Naomi's affects.

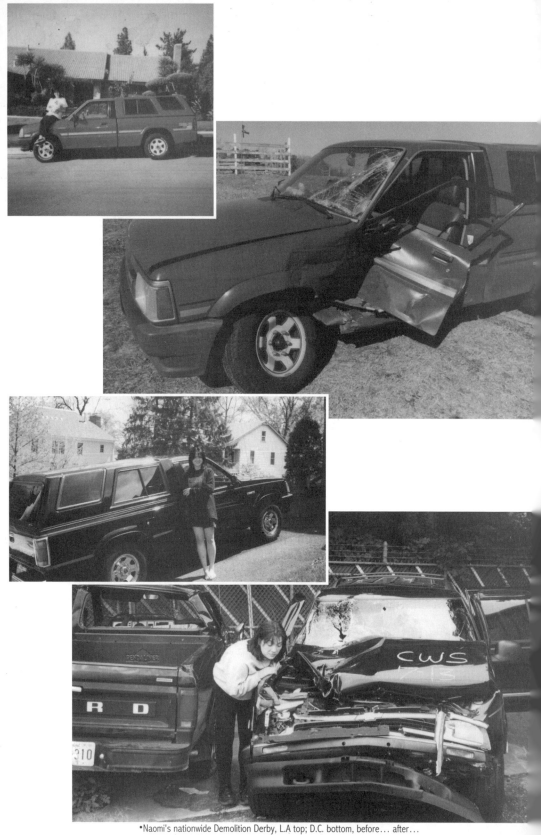

•Naomi's nationwide Demolition Derby, L.A top; D.C. bottom, before… after…

•Naomi, Los Angeles, March 1991. (Marco Mathieu)
•Marco, Chelsea, Naomi, Simi Valley, 1991 (CP)
•Chelsea & Naomi, Knotts Berry Farm, December, 1991.

•Raenie's in-house newsletter, Mail Order Madness, 1988. (courtesy RK)

HELTER SKELTER

GUNS DON'T KILL PEOPLE.
SONGS DO.

•Pettibon's Super Session Ten center-spread, 1992, STP Pubs.

•"Never." by Rosetta.

THIS IS YOUR ALL ACCESS BACKSTAGE PASS FOR

"THE LIFE O' LINDA"

MEMORIAL PARTY & FERRY RIDE

Come eat, drink and share thoughts of love, happiness & humor about Linda and her life

Saturday July 8, 2006
Lakeside Park in Oakland at 12:00 p.m.

The park entrance is at Grand Ave. & Bellevue Ave.
Look for blue & red balloons on the lake side of the park

At 4:45pm we will caravan to the Clay St. Pier at Jack London Square for the ferry ride

The round-trip ferry will depart at 5:45 p.m.
Linda's ashes will be scattered at sunset.

If you would like to bring a dish or beverage, please feel free

Any questions please call Heather @ 310~367~1578

SEE YOU BACKSTAGE!!!

*Linda's memorial service card, 2006. (Greg Ramirez, Heather Trudnich)

Medea got back she asked all the people who walked past
SST for spare change so she could eat. Unfortunately, she
asked the guys if they wanted blow jobs so I had to tell her to
stop. She got about $3. It looks like she'll be here for a
while. She's withdrawing and she keeps having fits of anger,
then she cries & shakes! At least she doesn't vomit all over
the place....

    I haven't heard from Henry but I talked to Chuck who
said he is acting strange. I didn't tell him what they told me
cuz I want to talk to Hank B-4 I take action. If Henry's
depressed I will help him because he helped me a lot when I
had it rough. I care for him and I'll be damned if he's gonna
kill himself and stick me with the job of answering his mail.

    I have just begun to consume a pot of coffee so I can do
some homework. Wait –
                  I CAN'T BELIEVE IT.
SHIT. Medea has just returned from 7-11 and she said she
met some guy who she 'turned a trick' with in Hollywood....
So Medea makes a 'date' with this guy for 7:00 (It's 6:00
now) but she invites him HERE!!! Wait – it gets better. The
guy is bringing two buddies of his so Medea can get $75.00!!!!
I thought I was safe from that shit here at the beach!! How
did she do it??!!! I don't care how she did it. There ain't no
fuckin' way its gonna happen here!!! But it's three of them
against just me and Joe! What am I gonna do? I'll write you
and tell you what happens. Stay tuned, Davo"
(DC, June 9, 1982)

I don't remember how that episode ended. Medea was actually fairly
nice to me, telling Greg on the phone what a good job I was doing for
him – she perhaps was struck by what was becoming of Greg's dream –
one she had been in on at the beginning and traded for the street itself.
I remember her talking a lot about loads, which if I remember was a
three pill combo that could do when one was out of heroin, and also the
Sybil Brand Institute for Women which she hoped somehow to avoid
returning to.

    Greg was working the phones from tour to get Medea out of SST
before we were once more booted from the south bay. Greg got Spot to
move back down and he kept badgering Medea about collecting on a
long-promised sexual favor. This didn't strike me as particularly
helpful but I figured he knew her better than I did. I'm just glad I
didn't know Spot was packing a rod. She asked me if there was
something she could do for me, I declined – did she mean like lick

envelopes? The Ginns bought them one way plane tickets to Cleveland where Lennie was from. Mr. Ginn drove them to the airport where they thanked him profusely before selling the tickets and catching a bus back up to Hollywood, where Lennie promptly overdosed, surviving but now brain-damaged....

Of all the punk-era casualties, Medea was the last anyone expected to still be among the living. But with her street skills, the way she looked into men one after another, she found the city utterly predictable. And this had kept her alive against the longest odds Los Angeles can throw in front of a girl. A few days after talking to Pettibon, on my way back to Wyoming I met Chris Petersen at a casino in Las Vegas to talk about his sister and her determined trajectory against similarly long but opposing odds. I would have lost both bets. Medea with her nightmare childhood... Naomi with her loving family...

A year after Naomi died, Chelsea's mom died in an accidental drowning. She was troubled and had moved from L.A. to Las Vegas to start over. The second time out to Henderson I sat with Takeyo and Chelsea and we talked about Naomi and when Chelsea mentioned her mother she smiled wryly and said, "My female role models." In this new new America Chelsea was a cheerleader in one of those enormous new high schools and just graduated. She'll work with her dad on her aunt's archive.

In addition to the better-known bands that Naomi shot, dozens, hundreds of these now dead bands are secrets still. When the German or Japanese reissues, or the wireless ring-tone file-sharing ecosystem, or the film documentaries, or Archeology itself allows their rediscovery by some future kids dropping out of their over-produced, over-sold pop hell, they will find this music as clean and pure as field recordings. It's the last music recorded in our world before noise-gates and digital delay replaced space and air with a virtual reality that promised a lie better than truth. Such kids then will find more images of those bands are credited to one Naomi Petersen than to any other photographer. It might be possible to chronicle eighties music in America by knitting together the regional work of a dozen photographers or better yet tapping the <u>Flipside</u> photo archive if it exists, but no single photographer's work would need less augmenting than Naomi's, and her chronicle would include so many excellent, unheralded, otherwise unwitnessed bands that hers alone is indispensable.

Rediscovered, these bands will be heard by more people than were there, as was true for blues, rockabilly, surf, garage, psychedelia, etc. And then the musicians will be seen as they were in those moments through the lens of Naomi's Nikon, through her American eyes. An appropriate action-epitaph for this music-loving, history-obsessed, death-haunted, boy-crazy, insomniac, workaholic, absurdist, auburn-haired halfie girl – granddaughter of a Buddhist priest – born in Yokohama, raised in Los Angeles... One of us.

21. Postscript

In those years I would record bands on a small tape recorder. Occasionally I listen to these old rough-sounding cassettes and it always startles to suddenly hear myself addressed out of the noise by the voices of Greg or D., or Laurie or Naomi... It really did happen and as Bill said it was a privilege to be involved. Somewhere, Henry said his only regret was he didn't get there earlier... When we flew that plane over Steve Wozniak's US Festival in 1983, it was referred to as a laughably Quixotic gesture in one of the reviews (Herald-Examiner I think). I showed the paper to Greg and he shook his head like he did and said something like, Yeah and when the audience grows they'll think it just happened magically....

    If Santayana is right that those who forget the past are doomed to repeat it then I'd gladly erase the tapes, break the records, burn the photos and forget all about everyone and everything so as to insure meeting them again and doing it all over. It was some serious fun. But Santayana belongs to the era of heroic national missions and their concomitant bodycounts. Fukuyama says history has ended, and that feels more true today. It sure seems as if that kind of insane ambition in music and art has gone extinct as well. Cutting through the yelping or growling of the various rock radio formats one still hears today the heavier ghost voices of Layne Staley and Kurt Cobain in rotation: "What you give is not alive." or "I don't have a gun." – faint platinum decadent echoes that followed nihilism. They hang around on the radio, I think, because kids sense from them that something happened once. Something bigger than today. Perhaps they can hear back through decadence, nihilism, pretense, hope... all the way back to Elvis' joy.

    This isn't about Death. Death is unavoidable. It's about Life, which we see and hear everyday, is quite avoidable.

Note to bands, record labels, distributors, magazines, etc....

Naomi lost two large caches of negatives over the years. Her brother Chris Petersen would appreciate hearing from anyone who has prints that Naomi made or were made by the record labels and bands she worked with. These images may only exist in the form of these prints. Chris and his daughter hope to assemble everything they can before culling the work for publication. They would appreciate hearing from anyone with prints of hers.

They can be reached at:

info@naomipetersen.com

Thanks.

Rather than wave a bibliography in front of you (Naomi forced me to finally read the Fitzgeralds, for instance...), I'll just list some of the best readily available books, magazines, and websites for further reading about the music world described herein.

Books
Babylon's Burning, Clinton Heylin (UK ed.; Viking)
Blight at the End of the Funnel, Ed Colver (Grand Central Press/Last Gasp)
Coloring Outside the Lines, Aimee Cooper (Rowdy's)
Double Nickels On the Dime, Michael T. Fournier (Continuum)
Fuck You Heroes, Glen E. Friedman (Burning Flags)
Fuck You Too, Glen E. Friedman (Burning Flags)
Get In the Van, Henry Rollins (2.13.61)
Lexicon Devil, Brendan Mullen (Feral House)
Life Against Dementia, Joe Carducci (Redoubt)
Make the Music Go Bang!, eds. Snowden and Leonard (St Martin's Griffin)
No Values, Robert Vodicka (M.A. Thesis, Univ. of Kansas)
Our Band Could Be Your Life, Michael Azerrad (Little, Brown)
Party With Me Punker, eds. Jordan Schwartz, Dave Markey (Abrams)
Planet Joe, Joe Cole (2.13.61)
Please Kill Me, Legs McNeil and Gillian McCain (Penguin)
Raymond Pettibon (Phaidon)
Raymond Pettibon – Plots Laid Thick (Actar/MACBA)
Rip It Up and Start Again, Simon Reynolds (UK edition only! Faber & Faber)
Rock and the Pop Narcotic, Joe Carducci (Redoubt)
Spiels of a Minuteman, Mike Watt (L'Oie de Cravan)
Turned On, James Parker (Phoenix House)
Waiting for the Sun, Barney Hoskyns (Bloomsbury)
We Got the Neutron Bomb, Brendan Mullen (Three Rivers)

Magazines
Citizine, Los Angeles, Cal.
The Rise and the Fall, San Pedro, Cal.

Websites
Alicebag.com
Alisonbraun.com
Commonthreadpunk.com
Flipsidefanzine.com
Home.earthlink.net/~ttrocc7007/
Hootpage.com
Ipass.net/jthrush/rollflag.htm
Jennylens.com
Markprindle.com
Meatpuppets.com
Myspace.com/karanoid
Punk-information.com/History.htm
Ratsound.com/early.htm
Shockersite.com

Films
American Hardcore
Decline of Western Civilization
DogTown and Z-Boys
Mayor of the Sunset Strip
Please Don't Be Gentle With Me
Punk: Attitude
We Jam Econo

≠

ADDENDUM

≠

LETTERS

Naomi wrote letters all the time, at first to record labels, fanzines, and bands that she was into but did not know. She came to know almost everyone doing good things in the world of music in the eighties and into the nineties, and she wrote most of them. Be some book to gather and annotate those letters, but who saves letters? – Jeff Nelson and me. She didn't, of course... After going through his letters for me Jeff said he thought emails aren't ever likely to carry the weight that a bundle of old letters can.

Naomi Petersen –

July 18, 1985
From Simi Valley, Calif. to Washington, D.C.

Jeff-
...I am anxiously counting down the days til I leave – 56! I hope I have opportunity to do more photos of things/people other than just bands over there. I just don't have the time here to do any creative stuff. Or perhaps it's just that I don't make the time – probably so, but I have been working an awful lot trying to save all that I can. I'm also poking away at my German studies....

»

October 7, 1985
From Minden, West Germany to Washington, D.C.

Jeff-
Wie Gehts? How's things back in the good ol' U.S.? I'm still loving Germany – I'm so glad I was able to get things together to come.... I haven't watched any television or read any American magazines or newspapers since I've been here (almost a month now) – kind of strange because as far as news goes, I don't really know what's been happening in the world lately except that Mexico had a terrible earthquake & that Rock Hudson died. Let me know if there's been any explosive news that perhaps I should know about. (Like if they've cancelled "David Letterman"). How's things with the label? The label here, Weird System, that I've arranged to do photos for is much smaller & non-professional than they seem in letters but for now it's OK. I'm just glad to be here. Lots of

Nazi/Skinheads here – it's really a big organization. The other night I saw a lot of them in the Hannover train station and some friends of mine told me that they go there to beat up punks because that's where many punks meet before gigs. Pretty sad to see such young kids with already twisted minds....

»

November 20, 1985
From Minden, West Germany to Lawndale, Calif.

Joe–
Hi – just got your letter yesterday. Europe is quite nice (especially Switzerland) but it's rather cold. It's already snowing. All in all everything is going well. I'm going to Poland on Sunday – should be real interesting I think. Well, I was really surprised to hear you say you're leaving SST – is this a permanent thing? I had planned on staying here til mid-January but in these past couple of weeks I was debating on whether to go back sooner. And after I got your letter, I decided that it would be best if I returned earlier. I think I'll enjoy myself more anyways not having to worry about having to make my money stretch for that extra time. And so, I will be back on the 22nd or 23rd of December – you can plan on me being ready & able to work on the 26th. I'll call you as soon as I'm back. I asked my mom about the color infrared St. Vitus slides that she was supposed to pick up for me – they took seven weeks to develop – but she said that she sent them to me – I'm anxious to see how they turned out. That reminds me, I went to the cemetery where Jim Morrison is buried last week. (in Paris) What a great old place that is. Anyways, depending on when I get the slides & how they turned out, I'll either mail them to you to look at or if the time difference isn't that great, I'll just bring them back with me. I hope all is going well – how's the new place? I'm rather looking forward to going back & working. Traveling can seem a bit unproductive at times – especially sitting around waiting for trains. But it's been a good experience. Let me know if there's anything you need. See you in about a month.
                                            – Naomi

»

November 28, 1985 (Gdansk Memorial postcard)
From Kartuzy, Poland to Washington, D.C.

Jeff-
Well, Poland is much like I imagined but it's good to be able to see it for myself. Yesterday, I went to Auschwitz & Birkenau. I can't really explain in words what it was like 'cause it just gave me a feeling – it was far different to actually be there than to read about these places or see them on film. I'm extremely glad I went – on this Thanksgiving day I can really realize all that I've got to be thankful for. I think it's my most meaningful Thanksgiving ever even if I am so far away from home....

»

December 3, 1985
From Minden, West Germany to Lawndale, Calif.

Joe-
Grüße! Just a quick note to let you know that I've once again changed my plans for returning home. My airline is a bit screwy and I'm having some trouble getting through to them to change my plane date to the 23rd and so I'm just going to go back to my original plan of going back on the 16th (of this month). So, you can now prepare that I'll be able to start working on the 18th. I'll give you a call on Tuesday the 17th to let you know that I got back OK & such and also to get directions to the new location. Seems like I've got a million things to do now that I've set a date that's coming up so soon but it's really definite this time. So, I'll be seeing you in a couple of weeks!
        Bis dahin!
        -Naomi

P.S. When I was in Poland – (a rather depressing place but full of interesting conflicts – I'm glad I went & saw it all for myself) anyways, when I was there one night on the radio they played the entire new Hüsker record. I, for one, was rather surprised. Just thought you'd like to know. *Ciao.*

»

October 14, 1986
From Lawndale, Calif. to Washington, D.C.

Jeff.
I'm back studyin' my German and I'm now doing freelance art/graphic work aside from photo biz, SST & Global so I'm keepin' pretty busy. The "Village Voice" (paper from N.Y.) has asked me to be their West Coast underground photographer (!!) and I'm pretty jazzed about that. Maybe someday I'll even get to leave my restaurant job for good... P.P.S. No news on my negs.

»

November 2, 1987
From Redondo Beach, Calif. to Chicago, Ill.

Hi Joe!
How ya doin'? Nice to hear from you & that you seem to be doing well. How's the house coming along? Sounds like a lot of work. Well, things have been looking a bit brighter for me lately – I got a new apartment in Long Beach that I really like (it's even got a darkroom) and now a brand new truck. I was in a wreck the day I found my apt. – I'm ok but my car was totaled. And today (well, tonite) I start a new part-time job cashiering at a restaurant (Bobby McGee's). I simply cannot live on what I get paid here – even at working so many hours a week. On my last paycheck I worked <u>126</u> hours in two weeks – I'm getting serious job burn-out. So I think working somewhere else part-time might break up the monotony. Besides, this new job is paying me more starting than

I've managed to make here in 2 years. I did photos of DOA, Dag Nasty & Nomeansno this weekend – all were great. I did stuff of the Tar Babies a couple weeks ago – I think they're a lot better now than on their record (they've a sax player now). Did you go see fIREHOSE and Slovenly last week? I heard Chicago didn't have a really great turnout. People here figured it was because of the World Series. Mike Watt got really sick after that and to be rushed to the hospital but I understand he's better & back on the road now. Who are your current SST favourites? I like the Tar Babies, Screaming Trees, Lawndale & the Meat Puppets, fIREHOSE, & Sonic Youth of course. My tastes have always leaned more towards the English/European sector. I hopefully will eventually move back to Germany or thereabouts – I really miss it. I'm looking forward to moving back east – I only hope that I can save enough to do so by the spring. I'm considering going to Australia for a couple of weeks before I move so I might have to postpone moving a couple months. I'm in no terrible rush to move but I do hope I'm not in Los Angeles another year – I've really had my fill of LA & the scene here. And also I feel, as I said, that my role here at SST has become rather mundane and with virtually no personal satisfaction from my day to day chores that I simply can't stand to keep going at this much longer – most times I just feel so unproductive. You're quite right, it's mostly become a job of maintenance. I'd like to just go back to doing free lance photos for them – Ray fortunately keeps me busy enough on that end that I do feel I play somewhat of a productive role in things & have a significant input into keeping things going. Well, guess that's about it for now. I hope all is going well with you in all that you're doing. Hope to hear from you again soon.

PS, Has Ray told you about Greg's new record label (Cruz records) and booking agency (Clockwork)?

            Take Care,
            Naomi

»

September 18, 1987
From Redondo Beach, Calif. to Chicago, Ill.

Hi Joe!
How're you doing? I've been meaning to drop you a line for some time now but something always seems to interfere when I start writing. So, how's your writing going? Do you miss working at SST? I think I'm going to be leaving in the spring. If all works out, I'll move to Virginia – hopefully around Arlington but perhaps down to Richmond. There I can afford to rent an entire house and be able to set up a proper studio & darkroom. At the moment here I can't even find an affordable apartment (even with me working at SST 50+ hours a week) – I've been rendered homeless – all my stuff's in storage – it's pretty much a real drag. I think I've found a roommate though so hopefully it'll be easier to find a place with two people. I'm really looking forward to moving back east – I've had my fill of Los Angeles. Also, things at SST just don't seem to be happening all that much for me – things & people have changed – as I suppose so have I. But Chuck is wanting to use less & less of my photos and more and more just treating me as a secretary and I find it all a bit stifling. Do you come to LA to visit ever? Do you still keep in touch with Greg & Chuck? I know you still keep in touch with Ray – Ray is really great – he's probably one of the biggest reasons I've stayed working here. Do you keep up with the Chicago music scene? My friends the Effigies just reformed with 1/2 of Bloodsport – I've heard they're better than ever. I like Naked Raygun a lot – I wish they'd come out here. Well, guess I should get going home – enough for this kid. Well, Joe, I hope all is going well with you and I hope to be hearing from you sometime in the near future.

            Take Care,
            Naomi

»

•June 20, 1991 - Sacramento.

•Naomi with 9:30 Club crew, early 90s - D.C.
•Naomi in the 90s.

•At gig's end band turns the camera on Naomi, early 90s (C.O.C.)
•Naomi, parents, Chelsea at Leroy's Utah State mural, July 24, 1993. (CP)
•Naomi late 90s.

•Left-handed self-portraits with subjects in the early nineties…

...the personal is professional. (NP)

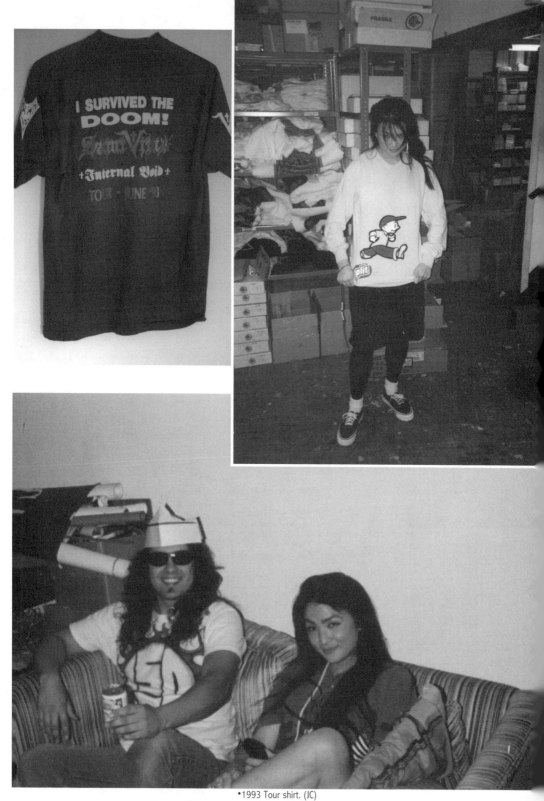

•1993 Tour shirt. (JC)
•Naomi at RAS; she wrote "Forever a Teenager!" on the back, Jan. 1993.
•Surviving the Doom, 1993. (c. Dave Chandler)

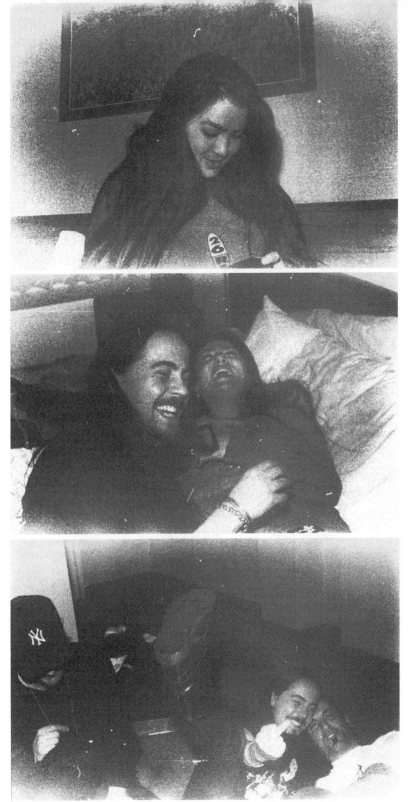

*Somewhere between Okla. and Colo. on the 1994 Obsessed/Unsane/Entombed tour; heat-damaged negs developed in 2006. (first 2 by member of Unsane, 3rd by NP)

•Noriko, Takeyo, Yoshitaka, Toshio, Iwao, Japan, Apr. 1998. (CP)
•Naomi center with parents at reunion in Japan, 1998. (CP)

•Bonding with halfie Colonel far from his plantation, 1998. (CP)

•Wedding Party, Chris and Chelsea on the left, Aug. 26, 1998.
•Naomi and John.

•2001, Winchester, Va., John visiting.

*Naomi Petersen by Brian Walsby, 2005.

November 12, 1987
From Redondo Beach, Calif. to Chicago, Ill.

Hi Joe–
Good to hear from you again. As I'm not doing anything particularly exciting at the moment I figured I might as well get you some flyers & photos together now – I don't know what photos you already have so I just grabbed one of whatever I could find. They seem to be out of quite a few bands. I saw Crazy Backwards Alphabet & Universal Congress of last week – it was really good. Universal Congress have gotten so good these past few months I can hardly believe it – I think the Saccharine break up has been really good for Joe. Jack Brewer has a new band called Sandbox but I've not heard them yet. They were going to play with Scream last weekend at Al's Bar but unfortunately Al's is closed down once again. Always August will be here next week – they're nice guys but I'm not really one for their kind of music. Well I'm glad that you've got the house done and have time to concentrate on writing – I'd really like to read some of your stuff sometime if you ever feel like sending something out. What's this book you're working on? Enclosed is a photo list – I'll try & get some contact sheets together for you soon of the bands that you mentioned that I have. Working 2 jobs plus photography is certainly getting tiring but it's not all that bad. Only thing is that I've yet to really set up my apartment – for the most part I'm still living out of boxes with things scattered everywhere. I'm cutting my hours down at SST to about 50 a week – as time goes on here I feel that my time can be better spent elsewhere and on other things. But I'm not going to quit til I move to the east coast – there really wouldn't be much point in trying to start up somewhere new when I know I'll be leaving relatively soon. Did you go & see the Divine Horsemen? I've been listening to a lot of European stuff lately – friends in Germany, Poland & Greece are sending me some new and refreshing records. I sort of like Laibach from Yugoslavia (especially the "Life Is Life" song/video) – actually I probably like them more out of curiosity than anything – they're rather interesting. Well, not much else going on – the fIREHOSE, Slovenly & L.Trains show next week should be good. I guess Mike is recovered from whatever he had – he and Kira are getting married on the 20th of December – did you know that? And Ed is

living with Nan, Mike's old girlfriend. Seems like everybody's getting married these days. (Scott – old Vitus singer – is now married as well) Hope everything is goin' well with all that you're doing. Hope to hear from you again soon.

        Take Care,
        Naomi

      »

March 2, 1988
From Redondo Beach, Calif. to Chicago, Ill.

Hi Joe!
How ya doin'? Sorry it's been so long since I've written – lot's goin' on and I was sick with a kidney infection for a few days which was a real drag to go through. I hear you've talked to Ray – I can't believe they fired him and then again I can – they're so ill now-a-days.... When are you comin' out to do the Vitus record? I went & saw fIREHOSE and the Alter Natives last night – was just soso. I saw Angst a few weeks ago and they were GREAT. Had a real good talk with Joseph. Oh, before I forget – yes I remember the negatives that I developed for you – I'm not exactly sure where I put them – my apartment is still very chaotic from moving – but I'll try & find them this week. I hear that Robo is going to do some sort of recording with ex-Misfits – I always wondered what happened to him. I had him pictured as working in a cigar store in some off beat town far off somewhere... *** is going to be a father – he seems quite happy about that. I wonder when the Watts will be expecting... (Be interesting to see their kids in a few years...) How's the writing going? Is the book you're doing going to have a lot of writing or will it be mostly photos? I'm going to go do photos of HR and Ras Michaels at the Roxy t'moro. I don't expect it to be very good – I find that HR is too preachy in his ras-ness. I think I might work for RAS records when I move out east – they're opening up to do some rock bands – starting with Scream as of May. Could be pretty good – Chuck & Mugger were already talking shit about me when they heard I was moving out east because they figured that I would automatically be working for

Dischord records and they "warned" me of giving them "confidential" information taken from SST: They're so fucking paranoid that everyone's out to "get" them... Glad I don't have to deal with them much anymore. Well, on to better, happier subjects – I saw Jeannine at the Meat Puppets gig a couple weeks ago – she seems to be doin' pretty well. They (Pups) played with a band called House of Freaks (just a guitarist & drummer) and they were really good – if you get a chance to see 'em sometime you should. This guy at the restaurant I work at is giving me a coffin – he got it from some playhouse – it was a prop – I'm thinking of making it into a phone booth (a la the Munsters) or a coffee table which would be really cool as the front of it is glass so I could put a mannequin in it or somethin'. It needs some work but I think it would be a cool thing to have around. Altho I probably wouldn't take it with me when I moved. Well, guess that's about it – I'll get to looking for those negatives for you in these next days. Hope all is goin' well with you.

        Take Care,
        Naomi

»

April 9, 1988
From Redondo Beach, Calif. to Chicago, Ill.

Hi Joe!
How ya doin'? I'm really sorry that I didn't get a chance to see (or even talk with) you while you were out. I tried to call you several times but I guess you guys spent a lot of time in the studio – I thought you might've stayed on a couple extra days after the record was done – how come you left so quickly? I heard part of the record today (sounded good) – we went & did a photo shoot out in Irwindale for the back cover – hope it went ok. It was almost 100° out there and Scott was wearing all his leather (!). Dave & Mark told me that SST was trying to steer them away from using me – it's funny 'cos when I go over there they're all nice & smiles but I hear a lot of shit that they say & do – I'm trying to associate as little as possible with them – I'm sure that's more than

fine with them. Dez was with us today – I guess DC-3 will be continuing as a 3 piece. I think they should get a rhythm guitar but Dez said he'd like to try it this way for a bit. Ray came to the restaurant I work at and we sat and did a Happy Hour thing the other day – it was good to sit and talk with him again – I guess he'll be going to NYC for a few weeks soon. So, how's the writing going? I'm going to be doing some artwork for a Fax machine company's office which I'm <u>really</u> looking forward to. I haven't done much artwork in the past couple of years and this should be a good opportunity for me. Plus I could certainly use the extra cash – I haven't been able to save hardly any money toward moving which is getting really frustrating. But I just got a raise at the restaurant so hopefully things'll be picking up. I now hope to be able to move by July but it might be better to wait til September – we'll see. Well, I hope everything's going good for you. Oh, did you talk to Greg & Chuck while you were here? I'm curious to know how they were towards you. Well, hope to hear from you soon.

P.S., No... his new girlfriend is Mexican and his biggest comment was: "I just hope the baby's white..."

Take Care,
Naomi

»

November 23, 1988 ("Life in Hell" postcard)
From Lawndale, Calif. to Chicago, Ill.

Hi Joe!
Sorry I haven't written in so long but I'm just workin' so much that I've hardly time to do much else... This past weekend Sonic Youth were in town & I thought were really great. Also notable were Mudhoney. I missed the new Jack Brewer band but I understand they're pretty hot so I think I'll go check 'em out in 2 weeks at the Anti-Club. U.C.O. are so amazing these days... Ray said that Joe is interested in being on Blast First but Ray is kind of wary of getting too many ex-SST-ers on B.F. (Too bad...) So, what have you been

up to? How's the book going? I went to SST today to pick up a couple copies of the new Bad Brains Live CD (I did the front piccie). Greg is really strange towards me. Oh well, I guess I didn't really expect much different. No big... Well, I hope all is goin' well for you out there. If there's any new SST stuff you want I can still get it at the "employee discount" so I'll pick up anything you're interested in. –K? Take Care. Happy Thanksgiving!
                                            -Naomi

»

February 9, 1989
From Redondo Beach, Calif. to Chicago, Ill.

Hi Joe–
How ya doin'? I'm working right now as a fill-in cashier for the evening – gotta start workin' a lot again to really save to move. What's new? I haven't seen Ray since the beginning of the new year (although I talk to him regularly) – he's been so busy with Blast First. Did he tell you he's going to Russia with Sonic Youth? I'm quite envious. T'moro I'm going to go see Nomeansno in San Diego. Should be good – I haven't been to a gig in a few weeks. Sunday & Monday I'm going to go see Jay Leno & Harry Anderson both of which should be great shows. Hopefully I'll be going to SF soon to do some photos for Opal. How's the writing going? Have you seen the new book "Banned in D.C."? It's pretty cool. It snowed in LA two days ago – I can't believe how cold it's been but I reckon if I'm going to be movin' to VA I'd better get used to it. Do you ever keep in touch with Spot? I wonder if he's still in Austin. Some goofy guy from SST called my phone machine the other day and said that Chuck said that it would be OK for them to use me as their "emergency" photographer – can you believe that!? No thanks. I said I'd sell them stuff I already had or do stuff for bands on SST that I personally know & like. Chuck & Greg have become a couple of real stuffed shirts as far as I'm concerned. Oh well.... Guess I'd better get back to business – hope that all is goin' good with you and to hear from you soon. Take Care,
                                            -Naomi

»

August 2, 1993
From Arlington, Va. to Minocqua, Wisc.

Hey Joe-
How ya doin'? Here at last is the full Unorthodox tape and a band on Relapse that I like, Dead World. Sorry it's taken so long and there's so much else that I want to send you but I simply don't have the time right now to make tapes and sort through with what I've got. This is my last month at RAS but I'm also up to my ears in booking Clutch, Thud, Internal Void, Who Is God? And trying to do photos and working out things with Relapse. Also I'm gettin' ready to go to school full-time in Sept. Which entails a lot more than I had anticipated. I am unfortunately not going to be able to go to SF for Ray & Isabelle's wedding – are you going? Well, I've gotta get to making some calls for this Clutch thing – hope you're well and to hear from you soon. Take Care
                                        -Naomi

»

March 3, 1997
From Silver Spring, Md. to Laramie, Wyom.

Dear Joe,
How ya doing? It was good to get your notice on your book signing. Have you talked to Henry lately? I haven't heard from him for about a year now. I heard that he fired everybody at 2.13.61... Oh well. I was hoping to talk to him about doing a photo book but I guess that's out – maybe one day... So, how's life in Wyoming? Do you like it better than Chicago? I went to LA for the holidays for about three weeks with my boyfriend. It was pretty nice. We went to Vegas and up to Frisco. We went to Alcatraz which was really interesting. I had lunch with Ray – he

seems like he's doing really well. I think that he mentioned that he and Isabelle are thinking about having children. My life has been pretty uneventful lately. A nice change from all the madness of last year! I don't know if I ever told you, but I got mugged and beaten up pretty bad last August. It wasn't fun. I almost considered moving back to LA but then I thought better of that. I don't go to many gigs anymore – I usually end up just being bored. I did however go see SHINE, Wino's new band, and they're really good. They play a lot of Obsessed songs as well as some new stuff. Wino's doing really good these days – he's been sober for eight months now (following an incident where he got so drunk that he beat up some guy and nearly killed him – I think he had to go to court for that last Monday). I hope he stays straight – getting out of LA was probably the best thing he's ever done for himself. Well not much else to report at the moment. I'm currently working for my boyfriend's father's plumbing company (John was my plumber – that's how we met) doing secretarial work and bookkeeping. It's pretty easy and I'm here alone for most of the day so I can get other things done (like catching up on letter writing). I hope that all is going well for you. Please tell me about this film that you've written... Looking forward to hearing from you soon. Take Care,

-Naomi

»

April 20, 1998 (Map of Japan postcard)
From Kyoto, Japan to Washington, D.C.

Jeff.
Konnichiwa, Jeff-San! I can't believe I'm finally back in Japan! I met with all of my relatives yesterday. It was great! They're very traditional people and to see that whole culture still exist in these times is really fantastic. I'm sure you'd really appreciate it too. Today we're in Kyoto – went by Mt. Fuji today (!) Tomorrow we go to Nara and then back to Tokyo & the region where my family lives. It's going to be far too short of a trip. Ah well, at least I'm here....

EUROPEAN TOURS - JOURNAL

Naomi also wrote notes on her calendars – usually big illustrated ones by Groening, Schultz, or Larson. She'd first fill in birthdays and upcoming gigs, then went back and filled in details about each day and those gigs. (Often, Naomi would emphasize her reaction to what she was writing with little line drawings of a smile or a frown under two dots for eyes.) She wrote most intensively in her calendar during 1990. She flew to Europe in late May of that year to catch up to several tours her friends C.O.C., D.R.I., and Prong were on with Faith No More, D.O.A. and others. For the first half of her two-week trip she kept a journal at the back of a weekly planner. This is the most extensive writing it seems she did; I wish I had more to pass along. It's her, in the moment, addressing herself, or us. I trust her friends won't mind my sharing this little glimpse of the Naomi roller coaster.

5.18.90

4:48 — Had an incredibly stressful afternoon with having spent all night organizing & putt-putting around and then having to work — finally got ahold of Geoff M, who said that he talked with Mike K. and they know I'm coming (whew!) but that they can't pick me up — so I guess I'll just try & call the promoter or whatever tomorrow. Never did hear from Reed, the Bugger. Jeff came over a bit early — wouldn't let him see my room cos of the chaos. Had a good chat in the car. He's going to see Mary @ Southern at the end of the month. Got to the airport earlier than expected so had a Stoli Bloody Mary 'n a beer so am feeling pretty relaxed by now. Sent t-shirt to Mark L the other day — really hope to have a letter waiting when I get home!! It's 4:54, just about time to board! I'm so excited! ps — am wondering about what's going to happen w/ Spike. Looking forward to seeing him again — hope everything's cool. Here we go!

5.19.90
6:26am — Well, have just had a slight breakfast on the plane — plane ride none too eventful and that's fine by me — even got to sit alone. Had a little bottle of champagne to kind of send myself off — put me off to sleep as well — which was a bit fun altho an unnecessary expense. Will be in Paris in under an hour! :) Ch was kinda cute guy — very French — to sit next to me but he had a dog w/ him so he moved — nice scorpion ring — oh well... Really getting curious about what things with Spike are going be like — hope he's glad to

5.19.90

See me God, this is already looking kind of sloppy - better practice a bit better penmanship! I just can't believe I'm doing this - whatever happens it's gonna be a great learning adventure. Can't keep from smiling...

9:30 am I'm sitting at LeGrimmer Chatelet having a cup of café au lait and not knowing what to do next. It's a bit early to call the promoter I should think. Would like to go walking about but gotta find a locker - hmmm...

11:21 am Took me forever to find a telephone that took coins instead of these cards they have. My bag weighs a ton & there are no lockers in sight. I seem to remember tho of there being some at L'Gare du Est. Well, tried to call the promoter, Salomon Hazot, but there was no answer. Also tried to call the venue, Elysée Montmartre, but also to no avail. It's pretty early tho I reckon. So here I am, at another eating establishment, drinking a very bitter sort of french bier, "33" Record, and am going to have a chicken salad, how adventurous of me... I don't want to go far from the post as I really want to get a hold of Prong or at least the promoter as soon as I can. I wonder where I'll be sleeping tonight?

1:08 pm Well - just spoke with Rick - road mgr. of Prong - whew! These very nice British gentlemen helped me to use the phone in here I go. Geeze - I'm gettin' really stoked. Here we go!

~3:30pm OK, everything great - really great - called Prong @ their hotel & went over a mess of stuff w/ Tommy Hobby - why did I keep thinking that Tommy's name was Mark?

5/20/90

3:56pm - Boy, craziness. Am presently on my way to Stuttgart - cos for one I was spending a ghostly amount of money in Paris, two, it's cheaper to go to Stuttgart than Munich, and three, I couldn't stand lugging around my bag anymore - it's really heavy and the straps are such so that it's not easy to carry. Anyway, did a quick photo session with Prong - Mike Kirkland is so fucking cute - anyways, which went really well. I had put all of my stuff in Tommy's room which was really cool of him. We went to the club which was in this really sleazy part of town - as was Prong's hotel - it was a really cool building tho. I went up to the sound board where Mike, the drummer of FNM was & he said "Hey, don't I know you?" - and he was REALLY REALLY nice - he knew who I was thru my pix and stuff - and we got to talking. Some French guy came up & talked with me for a really long time, he seemed pretty ok and I could tell he liked me - at the end of the night he kept asking what I was doing and I gave him one of my cards cos he wants to write me and I told him to see him at DRI/COC. I understand that their tour isn't going so well by the way - too bad - I hope everybody's in a good mood. I'm going to fucking kill Reed for not ever calling. I wonder how I'm going to find them tonite. All I can say is, I'd better. Be kind of fun to surprise them like this - I hope so, anyways. Well, back

5.20.90

to yesterday. Then I talked with Mike Patton who also was really cool but not as cute in person as I had expected. Oh well - we had a really nice chat. Also talked with Roddy from FNM who was also really nice. The only one I didn't like so well was Jim who seemed to have a bit of an ego problem. ~~Goo~~ Rick and John the managers were both really cool and got me passes and ok's to do pix from the sound board and up front. George, the merch. guy gave me 2 FNM t-shirts and a Prong shirt - cool! Forgot to get a black one so I'm gonna write Mike the drummer and ask him for one. Mike also said later that he'd really like to do a session with me — so I've got to call John Brassilian when I get back. Oh, George also took a keen liking to me and was quite sweet. I gave him one of my cards. Ugh, I ate some weird grilled cheese thing earlier and it's not sitting with me so well. Gotta watch what I'm eating - this'll be a good dieting vacation! Back to the show, so just kind hung around for a bit and Prong went on at about 7pm - so early! They were awesome even tho both bands had to keep their sound down. I got to take pictures from the barrier for 3 songs and during the 2nd song just as I was taking a picture of Mike, someone jumped on my head and I totally thought that I had broken a tooth. As it was I had only bit my lip but it was bleeding a bit and is a bother. Oh

5.20.90

It could've been a lot worse. Seems to me it took FNM a long time to go on and to tell the truth I didn't think they were all that great. They were good, but not as good as I had expected. Mike's a great drummer tho. They did a couple of really lame songs such as the Nestle's white chocolate song and they also played for what seemed a pretty long time. At the end, Mike said that they were all going to jam together in park so I could get a pic- and unfortunately, Tammy got "a fight with FNM's roadie on stage and it got really really ugly. I had the misfortune of being in their dressing room and Tammy yelled at me to get out. Oh, before the show I had asked everybody about doing a group shot and every- body was into it but this killed it. Oh well. Did a couple backstage of individual people, which was ok so I was just hanging around for the longest time and felt very much in the way. It was a bit weird cus I had all of my stuff in Cammy's room. Finally I asked Mike K. if I could stay in his room & he said yes. They went out to dinner with their record label and Norman, Wess and I walked back to the hotel. Ran into Mike from who I wished we would've hung out with. But we didn't and I went up into Mike & Ted's room and dumped my junk. Went out & got 4 beers — my god, every guy in front of those sleeze places tried to get me

5.20.90

to go in and then some bozo kept following me down the street with some roses and wanted me to go off with him. Yeah right. Boy, that whole area is really sick. Went back to the hotel - talked with the reservationist guy for a bit and then took a long needed shower. Went back out to get more to drink - got 2 more beers & a vodka tonic that cost 60FF! That's about $9 - not a fucking rip! Went back to the hotel, wrote a postcard and was pretty wiped out. I didn't hear Mike & Ted knock on the door for several minutes - they were kinda trashed and when they saw that I was on the floor Ted said I could share his bed. Mike said he was going to join us which would've been interesting but he didn't. Oh well... Ted and I got to talking and he put his arm around me and things got really cozy. Very sweet indeed. We didn't _ but almost. Was kind of weird with Mike in the room and all. We passed out. Woke up around 10 and Mike was up. He left and Ted and I talked some more. They'll be coming to DC again soon and he said he'd like to hang out. He seems like a really great guy. Well, we went out and I got them to do a photo session out in front of one of the sex stores by the hotel. I hope that some of it came out. Tammy seemed in a better mood, but not a whole bunch. They also really liked the contact sheet I brought from

5 20 90

the 9:30 show altho everyone seems to think that Mike looks impotent. We had a nice and sweet goodbye - Ted kissed me goodbye in front of Mike and Mike looked pretty surprised. I still kind of wish I had gotten together with Mike but Ted seems sweeter and I think we'll be seeing each other again. He gave me his address & phone # and said to call him if I ever go to NY. I'm getting several good reasons to have to go there - think I'll just have to do so soon. We just made our first stop, it's about 4:45 - we get into Stuttgart around 8:30. There are now a couple of rather noisy French people in the car who don't smell all that great. Ah well. I'm anxious about seeing Spike again - hope things are cool. I can't believe Reed - I'm sure tho he'll talk his way out of me being mad and blow it off... I just hope that I find them without too much hassel. So far though I'm <u>really really</u> glad I came. ☺

5.22.90
1:29 Well, we're on the bus on our way from Vienna to a beach in Italy - gotta stop writing cos the bus is running & it's too difficult.

5.24.90 -
4:41pm Well, I've not been writing like I had planned - oh well. Things are pretty good I guess. Right now I'm in ~~Pa~~ Padova, Italy - the show in Venice got moved. This place is huge - it's some kind of sports event place. OK, starting from Saturday. got to talking to this girl, Julie

•Naomi's journal, one week in October, 1990. (actual size)

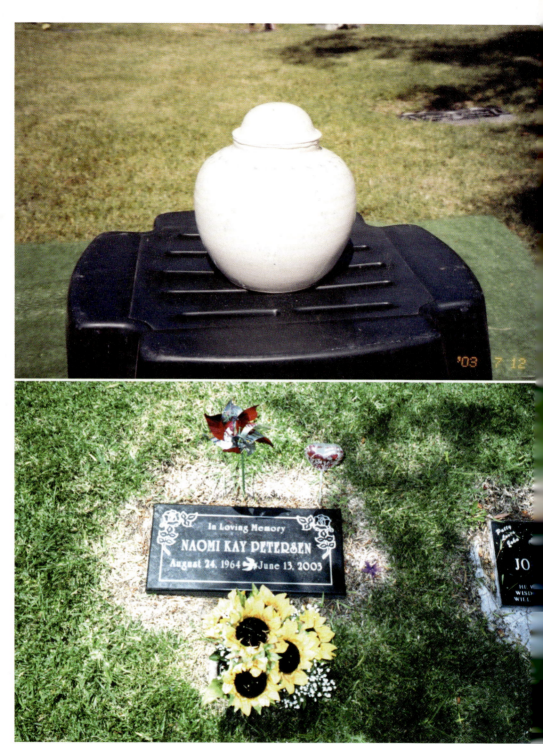

•July 12, 2003, Simi Valley Cemetery. (CP)
•July, 2005. (JC)

5.24.90

on the train who had a friend, Hugo, this black dance teacher, meeting here at the train station who lived in Stuttgart so I asked if he might know where the Longhorn was. Well he didn't but was really really cool & he took me to the ~~train station~~ club. It was really funny cos we were looking around - weird being in Stuttgart again. I thought about calling the Lohr's but I figured there was not much of a point of it. - anyways, I saw somebody in a DRI t-shirt so I told Hugo to stop and ask them and it was Kurt and Felix! I hopped out of the car and they were totally surprised, it was really funny. Anyways, got into the club and went up to the stage and called to Reed. It was great. Stupid fucking security people tried to pull me off but Karl told them to let me stay. Oh, as it turns out fucking Ron fucking stupid shit ass fucking Peterson never fucking told Kevin, the tour manager or anybody that I was coming! Stupid fuck. So DRI were totally surprised. Well, Spike knew and I ran into him on the stairs, really nice to see him again. I was pretty tired so I just went upstairs to the dressing room & sat with Spike and talked. He gave me a little kiss and was really surprised when I told him that I was staying on the tour for 2 weeks. He seemed a little aprehensive and said later that it was really going to be an "affair" and that his wife found out about the last time. Oh well. Anyways, great to see everybody - Reed & Karl were esp. sweet. Reed was under the

6.24.90

that everything was cool and of course as soon as I saw him I was no longer mad. So we just sat round and talked. Everybody warned me about the bus bathroom - pretty scary. Didn't watch Dri- will have enough chances anyways. On the way to the bus kissed Reed and it was sweet. Went to the hotel where Spike wanted us to get a room but Reed and Karl wanted me to stay with them. Well, soon as I got to the hotel, this really cool house-like place, Karl went to the bus. And, as soon as I got into bed, there were two twins, Reed crawled into bed with me! It was really really sweet and he kept saying how glad he was that I was here and now he'll have someone else to hang out with. Oh, before this, Kevin & Barry, the bus driver were making a really big stink about the fact that I was going to be on the tour cos they weren't told and things were really ill for a couple of days. Karl pulled Spike outside and they had a talk. Karl is SO sweet - All the band people totally stuck up for me and it was neat. Anyways, Reed and I just cuddled and stuff and fell asleep. We had to get up way too early to go to Munich. At the truck stop, I got to use some German and was pleasantly surprised at how well I'm doing with it. Got a bit to eat and Spike came in. He asked me what was up with me and Reed and Karl. I think he felt kinda weird. He said that Reed was giving him really weird looks when he saw us sitting together. Well, it was a bit awkward but I told him that I was

(oh took a fall on more direction from the steps on the bus - ow! I'm so clumsy!)

5 24 90

to kind of go out with Reed and that Karl's more like my big brother but that I had never slept with either of them. And Spike was really surprised. I mean, I never have actually been with Reed... So that all worked out we were on our way. Oh, everybody was right, the bus bathroom is sick. DOA were on the bill in Munich, at the Theatre Fabrik and I was really stoked to find that out. Got to Munich and there was still more fuss with me being here but and Barry said I had to pay him £150! Made me really sad. Karl said this that they'd pay for it and Felix went up and had a big discussion with Kevin and totally stuck up for me which I thought was really sweet. Got to the club and me and Karl went to the hotel to shower and stuff - nice to get things all sorted out. When DOA showed up I went up to John and we had a nice chat. Met Chris their new guitar player who was really cool. Joey was surprised to see me (seems like a trend) and I asked if they'd be into doing a group photo session and he said yes and also he said that they have a new live album coming out that they need a cover for. Killer! Did a few pix of the guys playing football and since Spike and John were gone doing laundry, we did a session with just COC and DOA which was pretty fun and then one of DOA - they are such nice guys. Saw Tomaso and went up and said hi to him & some other guy who remembered me but I didn't really remember him. Tomaso said that WX moved to Hamburg to this really political area where he's some radical

5.24.90

something or another. It figures. Gigi is in some other funk band and not really into hardcore anymore. Too bad, would've been nice to see him again. Well, the stage was really cool and I took pictures from above where the soundboard was and it was great. I think I got some good pictures of each band. Hope so - would be cool if I got one for the cover of DOA's album. Spike is letting me wear his pass thing all over. everybody now knows that we're hanging out. Anyways, after the show it was so great - I talked with Chris for a pretty long time - he's really really nice. Also got to talking with John who said his great great great or whatever grandfather was Brigham Young and we got to talking about Mormanism. We had a fantastic talk and he said he'd like to see me again! He gave me his address and I gave him a card. He wanted my Nirvana shirt really bad and I said I'd send him one. He was under the impression that I lived in Seattle and seemed genuinely bummed that I live in DC. I told him I might move to Seattle. I'm so funny. Well then, I managed to get everybody - except Phil - together for a big group photo session and it was just the best - I was so happy. Well DOA had to take off and Chris and John really wanted to hang out with us. wish they would've come back to our hotel with us. Joey wrote down all of their next dates and said he'd like for me to come to another of their shows. Wish I could but I don't think it's a possibility. Too bad. Well,

5·24·90

Kari was hanging around so it seemed a bit weird but when we said good-bye, I went to shake Chris' hand and instead he hugged me and gave me a little kiss. Very sweet. Then John gave me a big wonderful hug and we had a brief kiss. I think it would've been a bigger one if Chris and Kari hadn't been hanging around. Oh well. Hopefully there'll be other opportunities as a matter of fact I'm sure there will. — John seems really great – hope to see him again soon. Went back to the hotel and talked with Kevin. I was a bit tipsy and he said that Ron Petersen knew nothing about me coming on the tour – goddamn fucking lying bastard! I was SO SO SO SO SO PISSED! I said I wanted to talk w/ Ron and we went to call but Ron's phone was conveniently busy. FUCKER. Well, I was in a really sad mood after that and almost thought I was gonna cry. Woody gave me a really nice big hug and that helped and all the guys assured me that everything would be ok. — Well, I've got to stop for a while as my hand is starting to cramp up.